Contents

Contents

Sound/Spelling Cards
Punchouts

Name _____

Strategy Workshop

As you listen to the story "The Sandwich," by
Stephen Krensky, you will stop from time to time
to do some activities on these practice pages.
These activities will help you think about different
strategies that can help you read better. After
completing each activity, you will discuss what
you've written with your classmates and talk
about how to use these strategies.

Remember, strategies can help you become a
better reader. Good readers

- use strategies whenever they read

- use different strategies before, during, and
  after reading

- think about how strategies will help them

Name _____

Strategy 1: Predict/Infer

Use this strategy before and during reading to help make predictions about what happens next or what you're going to learn.

Here's how to use the Predict/Infer Strategy:

1. Think about the title, the illustrations, and what you have read so far.

2. Tell what you think will happen next—or what you will learn. Thinking about what you already know about the subject may help.

3. Try to figure out things the author does not say directly.

Listen as your teacher begins "The Sandwich." When your teacher stops, complete the activity with a partner.

What do you think might happen in the story?

_____

_____

As you listen to the story, you might want to change your prediction or write a new one here.

_____

_____

Name _____

Strategy 2: Phonics/Decoding

Use this strategy during reading when you come across a word you don't know.

Here's how to use the Phonics/Decoding Strategy:

1. Look carefully at the word.
2. Look for word parts that you know and think about the sounds for the letters.
3. Blend the sounds to read the word.
4. Ask yourself if this is a word you know. Does it make sense in the sentence?
5. If not, ask yourself if there's anything else you can try. Should I look in the dictionary?

Listen to your teacher read. When your teacher stops, use the Phonics/Decoding Strategy.

Now write down the steps you used to decode the word *peanut*.

_____

_____

_____

_____

Name _____

Strategy 3: Monitor/Clarify

Use this strategy during reading whenever you're confused about what you are reading.

Here's how to use the Monitor/Clarify Strategy:

- Ask yourself if what you're reading makes sense—or if you are learning what you need to learn.
- If you don't understand something, reread, look at the illustrations, or read ahead.

Listen to your teacher read. When your teacher stops, answer the questions with a partner.

1. What is Lionel's problem?

_____

_____

2. Can you tell from listening to the story what Lionel's problem is? Why or why not?

_____

_____

3. How can you find out what Lionel's problem is if you're confused?

_____

_____

Name _____

Strategy 4: Question

Use this strategy during and after reading to ask questions about important ideas in the story.

Here's how to use the Question Strategy:

- Ask yourself questions about important ideas in the story.
- Ask yourself if you can answer these questions.
- If you can't answer the questions, reread and look for answers in the text. Thinking about what you already know and what you've read in the story may help you.

Listen to your teacher read. Then complete the activity with a partner to ask yourself questions about important ideas in the story.

Think about the story and respond below.

Write a question you might ask yourself at this point in the story.

_____

_____

_____

_____

Name _____

Strategy 5: Evaluate

Use this strategy during and after reading to help you form an opinion about what you read.

Here's how to use the Evaluate Strategy:

- Think about how the author makes the story come alive and makes you want to read it.
- Think about what was entertaining, informative, or useful about the selection.
- Think about how well you understood the selection and whether you enjoyed reading it.

Listen to your teacher read. When your teacher stops, answer the questions with a partner.

1. Do you think this story is entertaining? Why?

_____

_____

2. Is the writing clear and easy to understand?

_____

_____

3. Did the author make the characters interesting and believable?

_____

Name _____

Strategy 6: Summarize

Use this strategy after reading to summarize what you read.

Here's how to use the Summarize Strategy:

- Think about the characters.
- Think about where the story takes place.
- Think about the problem in the story and how the characters solve it.
- Think about what happens in the beginning, middle, and end of the story.

Think about the story you just listened to. Answer the questions with a partner to show that you understand how to identify story parts that will help you summarize the story.

1. Who is the main character?

_____

2. Where does the story take place?

_____

3. What is the problem and how is it resolved?

_____

_____

Name _____

The Sandwich, by Stephen Krensky

Lionel liked peanut butter and jelly sandwiches.
He didn't like jelly and peanut butter sandwiches.

Make a shopping list for your favorite lunch food.

My Lunch List

What is your favorite lunch? Draw a picture of
your lunch in the tray.

Name _____

Choose the letter that completes the
name of each food. Write the letter on
the line at the beginning of each word.

| p | m | w | b | j | s | t | c | l |

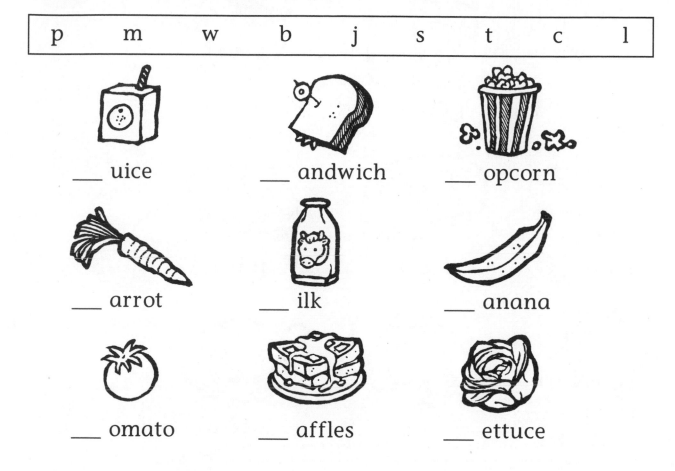

___ uice

___ andwich

___ opcorn

___ arrot

___ ilk

___ anana

___ omato

___ affles

___ ettuce

Writing Words You Know

Write a word you know on the line beside each
beginning sound.

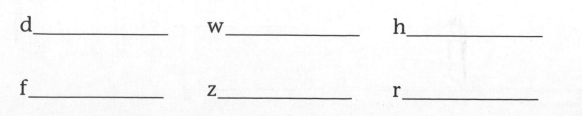

d_____   w_____   h_____

f_____   z_____   r_____

Name _____

Circle the letter that stands for the sound you
hear at the **end** of each picture name.

d t p   n d l   g p j

r l t   k s d   n b z

      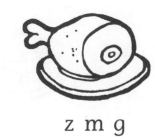

l r s   c t b   z m g

Writing Words You Know

Write a word you know on the line beside each
ending sound.

_____p   _____l   _____n

_____t   _____b   _____m

Name _____

Look at the pictures. Read the words in the box.
Write the word that names each picture.

stick	truck	drink
flag	clown	smile

_____   _____   _____

_____   _____   _____

Writing Words You Know

Write a word you know on the line beside each
beginning cluster.

br_____   fl_____   st_____

pr_____   gl_____   tr_____

Name _____

Write the letters that stand for the beginning
sounds you hear in each picture name.

br	fl	cl	tr	sn	cr	st

Writing Words You Know
Write a word you know on the line beside
each cluster.

bl_____   fr_____   pl_____

dr_____   st_____   gl_____

Name _____

Write **ch**, **sh**, **th**, or **wh** to finish each picture name.

tee_____   sandwi____   _____ip

_____eat   bea_____   _____irty

_____ick   di_____   clo_____

_____

Writing Words You Know

Write a word you know on the line beside each beginning digraph.

sh_____   ch_____

wh_____   th_____

Name _____

Write **ch**, **sh**, or **th** to complete each picture
name. Then draw a line to connect the row of
three pictures with the same sound.

pea_____   bu_____   _____umb

_____eep   _____air   pa_____

fi_____   _____orn   _____ain

Writing Words You Know
Write a word you know on the line beside
each digraph.

_____ ch   _____ sh   _____ th

Name _____

Complete each puzzle with the correct vowel. Then use the words to complete the sentences under each picture.

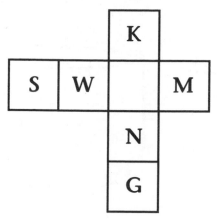

	K	
S W		M
	N	
	G	

The _____ can
_____ very fast.

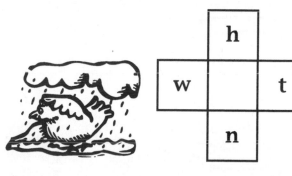

	h	
w		t
	n	

The _____ got
very _____.

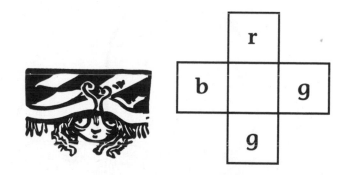

	r	
b		g
	g	

The _____ hid under
the _____.

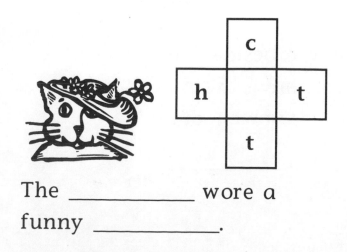

	c	
h		t
	t	

The _____ wore a
funny _____.

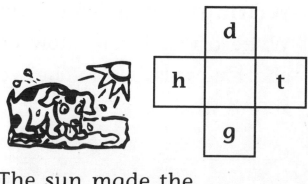

	d	
h		t
	g	

The sun made the
_____ very _____.

Name _____

Write a letter on a line to build a word that has the same short vowel sound as the picture name.

_____ an
_____ ab
_____ at

_____ ot
_____ od
_____ op

_____ ug
_____ up
_____ un

_____ et
_____ en
_____ eg

_____ ish
_____ ist
_____ ift

Writing Words You Know

Write a word you know on the line beside the short vowel sound. The word can have the vowel sound in it or begin with the short vowel sound.

a_____   e_____   i_____

o_____   u_____

Name _____

Look at the pictures. Read the words in the box.
Write the word that names each picture.

bee	flute	leaf
gate	goat	tie
vine	nail	rope

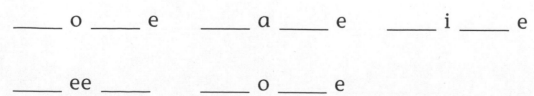

_____   _____   _____

_____   _____   _____

_____   _____   _____

Writing Words You Know

Write a word you know on the lines with the
long vowel sound.

____ o ____ e   ____ a ____ e   ____ i ____ e

____ ee ____   ____ o ____ e

Name _____

Add an *e* to the end of each group of letters.
Then draw a picture of the word you made.

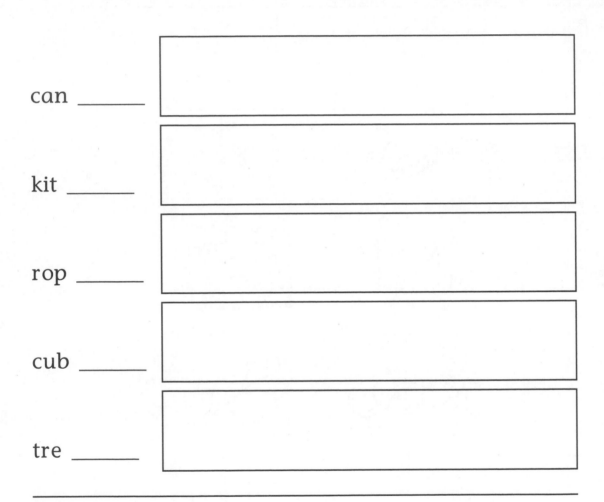

can _____

kit _____

rop _____

cub _____

tre _____

Writing Words You Know

Write a word you know with the long vowel
sound beside each vowel. The word can begin
with the vowel or have the vowel in it.

a_____   e_____   i_____

o_____   u_____

Name _____

Silly Stories

Write your own silly story. Think of a silly character, such as a plant or animal that speaks, then fill in the blanks to complete the story.

One day, _____

came into our classroom. It _____

and then it _____ .

Finally, my teacher _____ .

Now write three sentences that tell more about what happened. Then draw your silly character in the box.

_____

_____

_____

_____

Name _____

Silly Stories

Fill in the chart as you read the stories.

	Where do the silly stories in this theme take place?	What silly things do some of the characters do?
Dragon Gets By		
Julius		
Mrs. Brown Went to Town		

Name _____

Making Words

When you put these letters together, they make words.

m + a + p = map    p + i + n = pin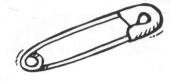

**Put these letters together to write words with
the short *a* and short *i* sound.**

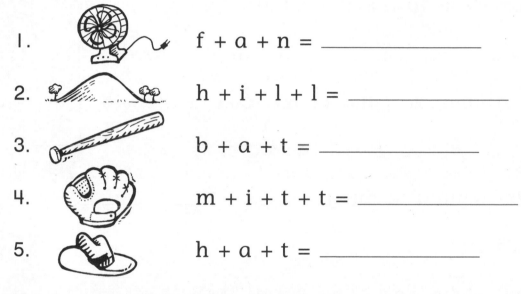

1.   f + a + n = _____

2.   h + i + l + l = _____

3.   b + a + t = _____

4.   m + i + t + t = _____

5.   h + a + t = _____

**Now use the short *a* and short *i* words you wrote
above to complete the sentences below.**

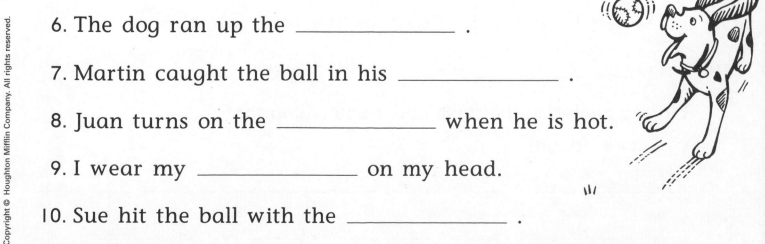

6. The dog ran up the _____ .

7. Martin caught the ball in his _____ .

8. Juan turns on the _____ when he is hot.

9. I wear my _____ on my head.

10. Sue hit the ball with the _____ .

Theme 1: **Silly Stories**   **21**

Name _____

Shopping for Food

Write the correct word to finish each sentence.

Word Bank

| bought | kitchen | roll | front | until |

1. Mr. Janson went to the store and

_____ many kinds of food.

2. He stood in line and paid for his food at the

_____ of the store.

3. Mr. Janson waited in line _____

   it was his turn.

4. He did not let his cart _____

   away.

5. When he got home, he took the food into the

   _____.

**Write a sentence that tells about something that
you have bought.**

_____

_____

Words That Fit

Use words from the box to complete the sentences in the puzzle.

Word Bank

hungry   vegetables   shopping   shopper   dairy   balanced

Across

1. If you are buying food at a food store, you are _____ .

2. Carrots, peas, and spinach are _____ .

3. Milk, cheese, and ice cream are _____ products.

5. A person who buys food at a food store is a _____ .

Down

4. When you need to eat, you feel _____ .

6. If you eat foods from the basic food groups, you have a _____ diet.

Name _____

Story Map

As you read the story, complete the story map below.

Who (Who is in the story?)

_____

Where (Where does the story take place?)

_____

_____

Beginning (pages 19–20) (What happens?)

_____

_____

Middle (pages 21–28) (What happens?)

_____

_____

_____

End (pages 29–30) (What happens?)

_____

_____

Name _____

Apple or Fish?

► Five Spelling Words have the short
  a vowel sound that you hear at the
  beginning of .
► Five Spelling Words have the short
  i vowel sound that you hear in .
► The words **was** and **I** are special.

Spelling Words

1. bag
2. win
3. is
4. am
5. his
6. has
7. ran
8. if
9. dig
10. sat
11. was*
12. I*

**Write the Spelling Words with the short *a* vowel
sound under the apple and the short *i* vowel
sound under the fish.**

apple

fish

_____   _____

_____   _____

_____   _____

_____   _____

_____   _____

**Write the two Spelling Words that do not have the
vowel sounds you hear in *apple* or *fish*.**

_____   _____

Name _____

Lightning Sentences

▶ A sentence tells what someone or something does.
**Write yes or no to tell whether each of these is a
sentence.**

1. Lightning struck the tree. _____

2. Rain splashes against the window. _____

3. A strong wind. _____

4. Dark clouds fill the sky. _____

5. We heard a loud clap of thunder. _____

6. We could see the lightning. _____

7. Shovels the snow off the sidewalk. _____

8. Snowflakes float to the ground. _____

9. Makes it warm outside. _____

10. The rain caused a flood. _____

Name _____

Who Is Dragon?

Read the questions in the circles. Write your answers in the boxes.

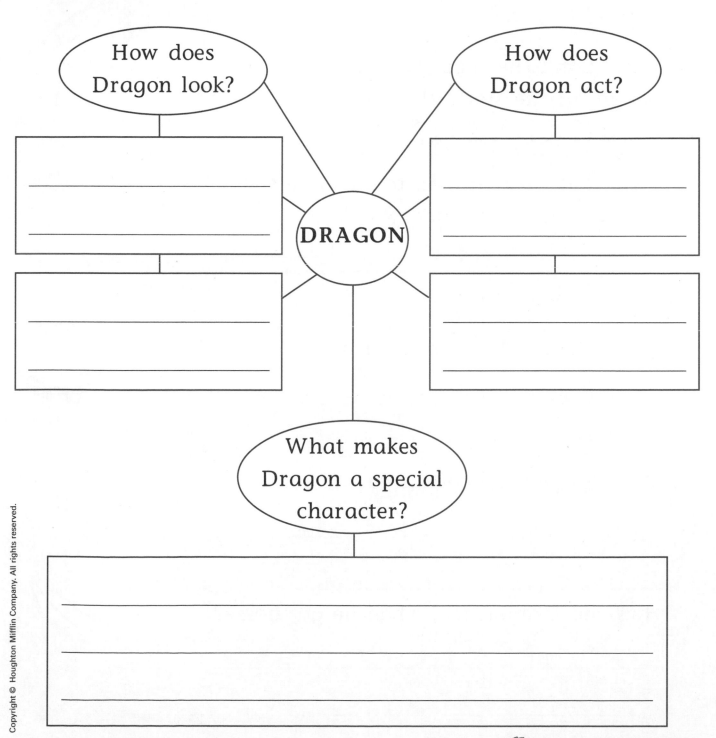

How does
Dragon look?

How does
Dragon act?

DRAGON

What makes
Dragon a special
character?

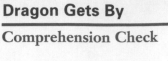

Name _____

Ask Away

Below are questions about the story _Dragon Gets By._
Write an answer to each question.

1. Why didn't the food that Dragon
   bought at the store fit in his car?

   _____

2. What did Dragon plan to do so he could
   fit the food in his car?

   _____

   _____

3. Why couldn't Dragon fit in his car?

   _____

   _____

4. How did Dragon get his car home?

   _____

   _____

5. How did Dragon feel when he got home?

   _____

   _____

Story Structure

**Read the story and then answer the
questions on the next page.**

Raccoon's Party

Raccoon wanted someone to talk to,
but he lived alone. He decided to have
a party. He put up balloons and made
some good food. He invited a few friends
to come to his party. Soon his friends were
ringing the doorbell. Raccoon asked them
into his house. He enjoyed talking to his
friends. It wasn't long before they didn't have
anything else to say to each other. It was too
early for the party to end, so Raccoon invited
more friends to his party.

Lots of Raccoon's friends came to his party.
Everyone was having a great time. That is,
everyone except Raccoon. The house was so
crowded, Raccoon could barely move. The
party was so noisy that Raccoon couldn't
talk to any of his friends. Raccoon knew what
to do. He wiggled his way past everyone to
the front door and stepped out of his house.
He was glad to be outside where he could
finally get some peace and quiet!

Story Structure continued

**After you've read the story, answer
each question below.**

Who (Who is in the story?)

1. _____

2. _____

Where (Where does the story take place?)

3. _____

Beginning (What happens?)

4. _____

5. _____

Middle (What happens?)

6. _____

7. _____

8. _____

9. _____

End (What happens?)

10. _____

Name _____

Spelling Spree

Word Clues Write a Spelling Word that answers each clue.

1. Something to carry things in _____

2. Something you do with a shovel

   _____

3. A word that can be found in **ham**, **jam**,

   Pam, and **Sam** _____

4. This word has only one letter

   _____

5. Add **h** to the beginning of **as** to

   make this word _____

6. Add **w** to the beginning of **as** to

   make this word _____

7. The word **is** can be found inside

   this word _____

8. A word that rhymes with **cat** and

   rat _____

Name _____

Pairs of Pears

Draw a line from each word on the left to a word on the right that sounds the same but has a different meaning.

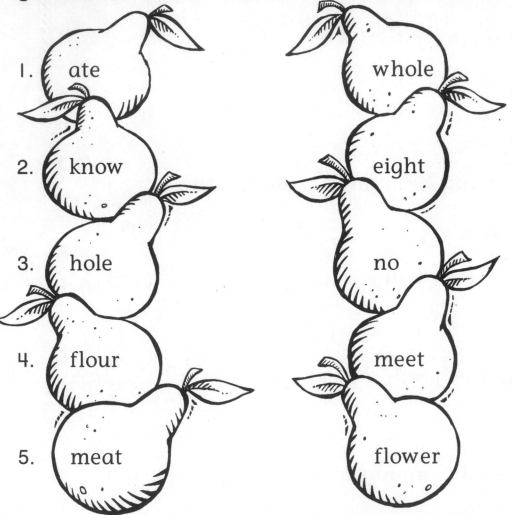

1. ate

2. know

3. hole

4. flour

5. meat

whole

eight

no

meet

flower

Choose one of the pairs of words. Write two sentences.

Use one of the words in each sentence.

_____

_____

_____

Name _____

Shopping for Endings

Example:

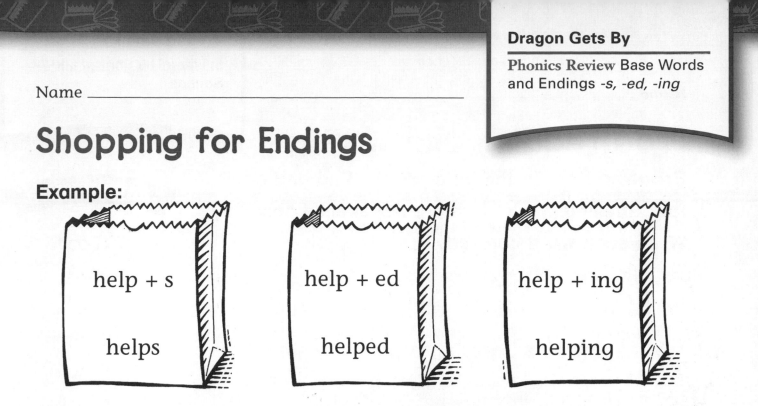

help + s

helps

help + ed

helped

help + ing

helping

**Look at each base word and ending. Put each base word
together with an ending to make a new word. Write the
new word on the line. Then read the new word.**

1. work   **+ s**   **+ ed**

   _____   _____

2. play   **+ s**   **+ ed**

   _____   _____

3. talk   **+ ed**   **+ ing**

   _____   _____

4. eat   **+ s**   **+ ing**

   _____   _____

5. stay   **+ s**   **+ ing**

   _____   _____

Name _____

Proofreading and Writing

Proofreading In the letter below, find and circle four Spelling Words that are not spelled correctly. Write each word correctly.

Dear Chris,

   I play on a baseball team. Our team name iz the Dragons. My hat has a picture of a dragon on it! I play third base. Iff we win our next two games, we will be in first place. I sat out today's game. My knee wus hurting. I hope I can play next week, and I hope the Dragons wen!

   Your friend,

   Bob

1. _____   3. _____

2. _____   4. _____

Write a Letter Write a letter to one of your friends. Tell about something that has happened to you. Write your letter on another sheet of paper. Use Spelling Words from the list.

Follow the Sentence Road

A sentence tells what someone or something does.

**Find the store by coloring only the pieces
of the road that are complete sentences.**

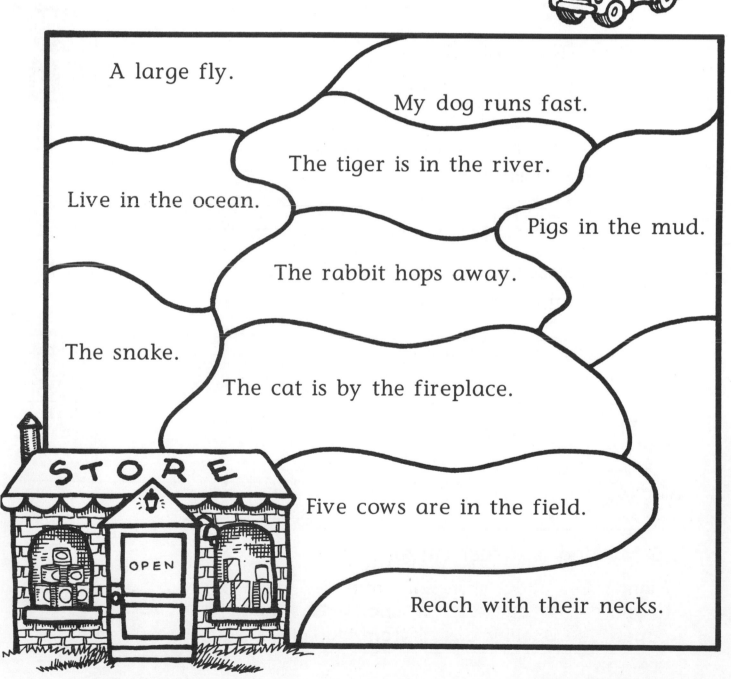

A large fly.

My dog runs fast.

The tiger is in the river.

Live in the ocean.

Pigs in the mud.

The rabbit hops away.

The snake.

The cat is by the fireplace.

STORE

OPEN

Five cows are in the field.

Reach with their necks.

Theme 1: **Silly Stories**　　35

Name _____

Telling More

Read each sentence. Rewrite the sentences so they tell more about the characters.

Example: David likes to write.

David likes to write long, silly stories.

1. Jessie has long hair.

_____

_____

2. The horse is wild.

_____

_____

3. The woman is strong.

_____

_____

4. The ape is silly.

_____

_____

5. My dog is a fast runner.

_____

_____

Name _____

Cans of Sentences

Circle the cans that have sentences.

mom bought two cans of soup

places the cans in the cupboard

we ate the peaches in this can

a can fell off the shelf

opened the can of peas

he put six cans on the shelf

cans of green beans

the labels tell what is inside each can

Write each sentence you circled. Remember to use capital letters and periods.

1. _____

2. _____

3. _____

4. _____

5. _____

Name _____

Revising Your Story

Decide how to make your story better. Put a check next to the sentences that tell about your story.

Superstar

☐ I wrote a beginning, middle, and end.

☐ My story has many interesting details about the characters and their problem.

☐ My story has a good title.

☐ I used words that say what I mean

☐ My story grabs my reader's attention.

☐ I wrote complete sentences, and there are few mistakes.

Rising Star

☐ There is no beginning, middle, or end.

☐ My story needs more details.

☐ I need to add a good title to my story.

☐ I didn't always say what I mean.

☐ I didn't grab my reader's attention.

☐ Some of my sentences aren't complete. There are many mistakes.

Writing Sentences

A Funny Clown Read each sentence. Write the parts of the sentence on the lines.

1. The clown ran around the ring.

   Who or What? _____

   What happened? _____

2. The clown jumped up and down.

   Who or What? _____

   What happened? _____

3. The little dog chased the clown.

   Who or What? _____

   What happened? _____

Write one or two sentences to finish the story.

_____

_____

_____

Spelling Words

These Spelling Words are words that you use in your writing. Look carefully at how they are spelled. Write the missing letters in the Spelling Words below. Use the words in the box.

1. w____s

2. m____

3. s_____d

4. th_____

5. h_____e

6. ____ny

7. th____

8. wi_____

9. i____

10. a____

11. y_____

12. o_____

Write the Spelling Words below.

_____   _____

_____   _____

_____   _____

_____   _____

_____   _____

_____   _____

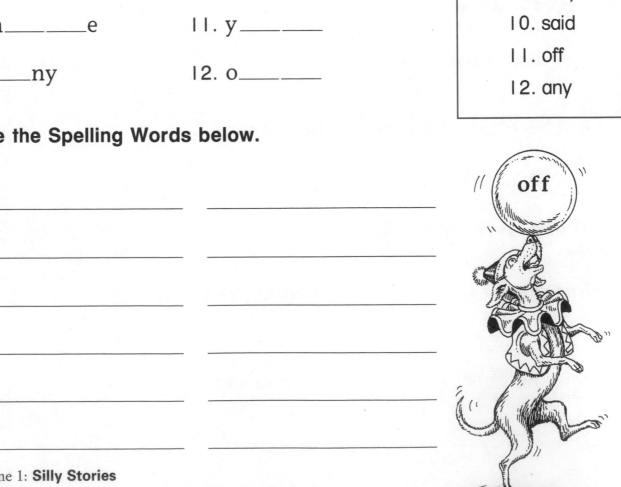

Name _____

Spelling Spree

Use the Spelling Words to complete the sentences. Write the words in the circus tent.

1. He ____ happy to go to the circus.
2. He wanted to see ____ clowns.
3. They ____ be funny.
4. Do ____ think the show will start on time?
5. "Yes, ____ will begin at six o'clock," said Tom.
6. Are there ____ elephants in the show?
7. "No, ____ are coming tomorrow."
8. We will ____ to come back to see them.

Spelling Words

1. the
2. will
3. it
4. have
5. as
6. my
7. was
8. you
9. they
10. said
11. off
12. any

1. _____   5. _____

2. _____   6. _____

3. _____   7. _____

4. _____   8. _____

Write the Spelling Words that rhyme with *sky* and *jazz*.

9. _____   10. _____

Proofreading and Writing

Proofreading Find and circle misspelled Spelling Words in this story. Then write each word correctly.

Spelling Words

1. the
2. will
3. it
4. have
5. as
6. my
7. was
8. you
9. they
10. said
11. off
12. any

Holly wuz the Walls's funny little kitten. Thay liked to watch her get up on her hind legs and dance around. One day she hopped into an open bureau drawer and fell asleep.

Brianna Wall came into the room. "I haf to get my new shorts," she sed. She opened the drawer and Holly jumped up. Brianna was surprised! Then the drawer fell. The clothes landed on the floor. Holly ran of!

1. _____ 2. _____ 3. _____

4. _____ 5. _____

Write Funny Sentences Write sentences about funny things or something that happens that is funny. Use as many Spelling Words as you can in your sentences.

Name _____

This Little Piggy

Write each word from the Word Bank under the pig that has the matching vowel sound.

Word Bank

hog   enjoy   mud   pigpen   grunt   hot

bed   box   cup

_____   _____   _____

_____   _____   _____

Finish the sentences below. Use the words from the Word Bank.

1. Pigs live in a _____ near the barn.

2. They make a sound like a _____.

3. Sometimes pigs get _____ in the sun.

4. They lie in _____ to stay cool.

5. Pigs _____ the way it feels.

6. A pig can also be called a _____.

Name _____

Pick a Pet

Write a word from the box to complete each sentence.

Word Bank

| brought | reason | special | surprise |

1. One day Mom _____ home a kitten.

2. It was a big _____ to everyone in the family.

3. The _____ Mom got the kitten was that she wanted a pet.

4. She thought the kitten was _____ because it had blue eyes.

What kind of pet would you like to have? Draw a picture of it. Write a sentence to tell why it would be a special pet.

_____

_____

_____

Name _____

Mind Your Manners

Living with other people can be difficult. Here are some rules to help everyone get along. Use the vocabulary words to complete the sentences.

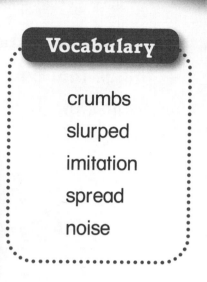

crumbs

slurped

imitation

spread

noise

1. Use a broom to sweep up cookie

   _____ on the floor.

2. Turn the radio low to keep the

   _____ down.

3. Keep your toys in one place so they are

   not _____ out.

4. After you have _____
   a drink, say "Excuse me!"

5. If you act like an animal, do the

   _____ outside.

Think about the rules at home. Write one of the rules on the lines.

_____

_____

Name _____

Fantasy and Realism Chart

Use the chart below to help you keep track of things that could really happen and things that could not.

Could Really Happen	Could Not Really Happen
_____	_____
_____	_____
_____	_____
_____	_____
_____	_____
_____	_____
_____	_____
_____	_____

Name _____

What's the Sound?

► The vowel sound in **job** and **pop** is called the short **o** sound. The short **o** sound may be spelled **o**. The words **from** and **of** are special. The vowel **o** does not spell the short **o** sound.

► The vowel sound in **pet** and **leg** is called the short **e** sound. The word **any** is special. The short **e** sound is not spelled with the vowel **e**.

► The vowel sound in **nut** and **rug** is called the short **u** sound.

Write each Spelling Word under the pet with the matching vowel sound.

Spelling Words

1. fox
2. wet
3. nut
4. job
5. leg
6. fun
7. went
8. mop
9. hug
10. from*
11. any*
12. of *

short o

short u

short e

_____   _____   _____

_____   _____   _____

_____   _____   _____

Now write the 3 words with the * beside them.

_____   _____

Theme 1: **Silly Stories**   **47**

Name _____

Who or What?

▶ A sentence is a group of words that tells what someone or something did or does.

▶ The naming part of a sentence tells whom or what the sentence is about.

Word Bank

| milk | floor | mop | fox | cup |

**Look at the picture. Then read each sentence.
Write the naming part to complete the sentence.**

1. A _____ fell off the table.

2. The _____ spilled out.

3. The _____ has to clean up the mess.

4. A _____ will soak up the milk.

5. Then the _____ will be clean again.

Name _____

Getting Ready to Respond

Use the chart to help you write a response journal entry about the story _Julius_.

What is the date?

_____

What is the title of the story?

_____

Who is the main character?

_____

What do you like best about the story?

_____

_____

Would you tell a friend to read the story?

_____

What example from the story explains why you like it?

_____

_____

Name _____

Hidden Message

Use the clues to complete the puzzle.

1. Julius made big _____ .
2. Julius and Maya went to the store to try on _____ , hats, and shoes.
3. They loved to _____ to jazz records.
4. Julius loved to eat peanut butter from a _____ .
5. Mom and Dad said Julius made too much _____ .
6. Maya taught Julius good _____ .
7. Maya and Julius liked to _____ at the playground.

1. __ __ __ __ __ ☐
2. __ __ __ __ __ ☐ __
3. __ __ __ ☐ __
4. __ __ ☐
5. __ __ __ __ ☐
6. __ __ __ ☐ __
7. __ __ __ ☐

Write the letters from the boxes to find out what Maya and Julius taught each other.

Fantasy and Realism

Read the story below and then answer the questions on the next page.

A Picnic in the Park

It was such a nice day, Gloria decided to go to the park. She packed a picnic. Then she called her dog, Ben.

"Let's go to the park, Ben. I packed a picnic for us." Ben came running. He stopped in front of Gloria. Ben gave her a big dog lick.

"I love the park," Ben said. "What did you pack for me to eat?"

"I packed your favorite dog food and some bones," answered Gloria.

"This is going to be a great day!" said Ben. He put on his sunglasses. "I can hardly wait to go down the slide. And I'll push you on the swing."

Ben ran to get some things he wanted to take to the park. He got his swim fins and a big towel. He got his best ball and a good book to read.

"Ben, you don't need all that stuff!" Gloria said. "Yes I do!" Ben answered.

"Okay, but you forgot the most important thing," Gloria said.

"My leash! I'll get it!" cried Ben.

Theme 1: **Silly Stories**   51

Name _____

Fantasy and Realism continued

Answer the questions. Use complete sentences.

1. Which character could be real?

   _____

2. Which character does make-believe things?

   _____

3. Name three things in the story that are make-believe.

   _____

   _____

   _____

4. Name three things in the story that are real.

   _____

   _____

   _____

What do you think Gloria and Ben will do at the park? On another sheet of paper, write an ending for the story.

Spelling Spree

Word Groups Think about the meaning of each group of words. Write the Spelling Word that goes with each group.

1. broom, rake, _____

2. bear, wolf, _____

3. arm, foot, _____

4. all, some, _____

5. bean, grape, _____

6. work, office, _____

7. gone, left, _____

8. hold, squeeze, _____

Spelling Words

1. fox
2. wet
3. nut
4. job
5. leg
6. fun
7. went
8. mop
9. hug
10. from*
11. any*
12. of*

Write a sentence using one of the Spelling Words that didn't go with any of the groups.

9. _____

_____

Name _____

Means the Same

Word Bank

| hat | ship | bag | plate | wash | start |

In each ball, write a word from the box that means the same or almost the same as the word in the ball.

6. sack _____

1. clean _____

2. dish _____

3. boat _____

5. begin _____

4. cap _____

Name _____

Pet Show

Mrs. Johnson's class had a show-and-tell about pets.
Read the rhymes to find out about the animals at the
show. Write words from the box to complete the rhymes.

Word Bank

| ants | cat | rabbit | fish | pig |

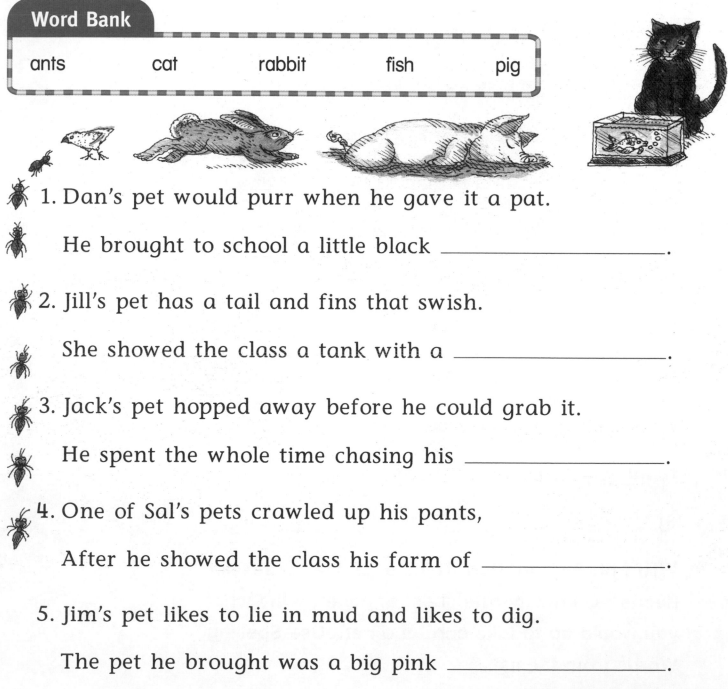

1. Dan's pet would purr when he gave it a pat.

   He brought to school a little black _____.

2. Jill's pet has a tail and fins that swish.

   She showed the class a tank with a _____.

3. Jack's pet hopped away before he could grab it.

   He spent the whole time chasing his _____.

4. One of Sal's pets crawled up his pants,

   After he showed the class his farm of _____.

5. Jim's pet likes to lie in mud and likes to dig.

   The pet he brought was a big pink _____.

Name _____

Proofreading and Writing

Proofreading Circle four Spelling Words that are wrong in this letter.

Dear Grandmother,

I have a new dog. His name is Josh. He is funn to play with. Josh likes to run frm one side of the yard to the other. Sometimes it is a big job to take care uf Josh. He likes to sit in his water dish. He gets all weet. Then he shakes himself.

Love,

Rita

Spelling Words

1. fox
2. wet
3. nut
4. job
5. leg
6. fun
7. went
8. mop
9. hug
10. from*
11. any*
12. of *

Write each word you circled. Spell the word correctly.

1. _____ 2. _____

3. _____ 4. _____

✏️ **Write an Explanation** Think of all the care a pet needs. On a separate sheet of paper, write what you would do to take care of a pet. Use Spelling Words from the list.

Name _____

Animal Manners

Word Bank

| fly | fox | bear | bees | kangaroo |

Write the naming word from the box that rhymes with the word in dark print in the sentences below.

1. These _____ say **please** when they ask for something.

2. A _____ asks what a guest would like to **do**.

3. The _____ says **good-bye** before hanging up the phone.

4. A _____ likes to **share** toys.

5. That _____ picks up his **socks**.

Name _____

Date It!

Rewrite the journal entry on the lines below. Write the circled words correctly.

(3 March 2001)

    I read the story (Lost in the park.) The main

character in this story was Connor. My favorite part

was when he found his mother. I like it because (connor)

was brave. Even though he was scared, he didn't cry. I

am going to tell a friend to read this story because it

is a very good story.

_____

_____

_____

_____

_____

Name _____

You're Last

Rewrite each of the sentences. Name yourself last.

1. I and Casey went swimming.

_____

2. I and my friend are going to the movies.

_____

3. I and my mother ate lunch at school.

_____

Draw a picture of you and your friend doing something.

Write a sentence to go with your picture.

Name _____

Long Vowel Game

**Read the sentences. Draw a circle around each word
that has a long vowel sound and that ends with silent *e*.**

1. We would like to play a game with you.

2. You count to five while we look for a place to hide.

3. When you count, you need to face the gate.

4. We can play until it is time to go inside.

**Now write each word you circled under the word that
has the same vowel sound and that ends with silent *e*.**

late   nine

_____   _____

_____   _____

_____   _____

_____   _____

_____   _____

Name _____

Chicken Riddle

Use words from the box to finish the sentences.

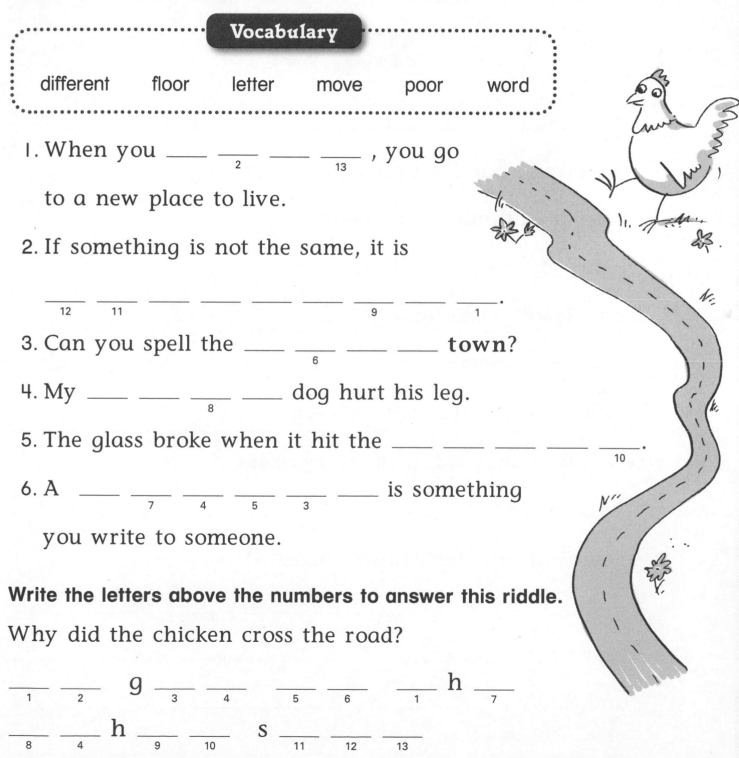

> ### Vocabulary
>
> different   floor   letter   move   poor   word

1. When you ___ ___ ___ ___ , you go
   ₂   ₁₃

   to a new place to live.

2. If something is not the same, it is

   ___ ___ ___ ___ ___ ___ ___ ___ .
   ₁₂   ₁₁   ₉   ₁

3. Can you spell the ___ ___ ___ ___ **town**?
   ₆

4. My ___ ___ ___ ___ dog hurt his leg.
   ₈

5. The glass broke when it hit the ___ ___ ___ ___ ___ .
   ₁₀

6. A ___ ___ ___ ___ ___ is something
   ₇   ₄   ₅   ₃

   you write to someone.

Write the letters above the numbers to answer this riddle.

Why did the chicken cross the road?

___ ___ g ___ ___ ___ ___ ___ h ___
₁   ₂   ₃   ₄   ₅   ₆   ₁   ₇

___ ___ h ___ ___ s ___ ___ ___
₈   ₄   ₉   ₁₀   ₁₁   ₁₂   ₁₃

Name _____

Picture the Vocabulary

Write each word from the box next to its correct definition.

Vocabulary

commotion   released   delivered   tire   feathers   wearing

1. something handed over to someone _____

2. having clothing on the body _____

3. light, soft parts of a bird _____

4. having set something free _____

5. noisy excitement _____

6. to have little strength or energy _____

Now use the picture to finish these sentences.

7. As soon as the _____ was

   released, the **commotion** began. First,

   _____

   and then, _____

   and finally, _____

   _____

Name _____

Prediction Chart

As you read the story, complete the chart.

What happens in the story?
_____
_____
_____
_____
What would happen if . . . ? _____
_____
Tell what happens. _____
_____
What would happen if . . . ? _____
_____
Tell what happens. _____
_____

Theme 1: **Silly Stories**   63

Name _____

Sorting Spelling Words

Ten Spelling Words have a long vowel sound and end with silent *e*. The words **give** and **have** do not follow this rule. The letters follow the pattern, but the words do not have long vowel sounds.

Write each word in the box under the word with the same vowel sound.

bike

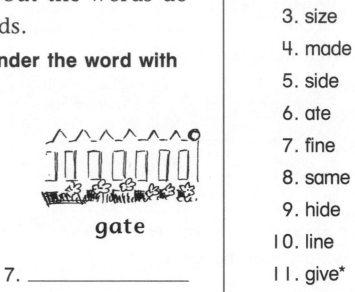

gate

1. _____

2. _____

3. _____

4. _____

5. _____

6. _____

7. _____

8. _____

9. _____

10. _____

Write the Spelling Word that answers each question.

11. Which word rhymes with **live**? _____

12. Which word starts with a vowel?

Name _____

Action Parts Puzzle

Color the puzzle pieces with action parts red.

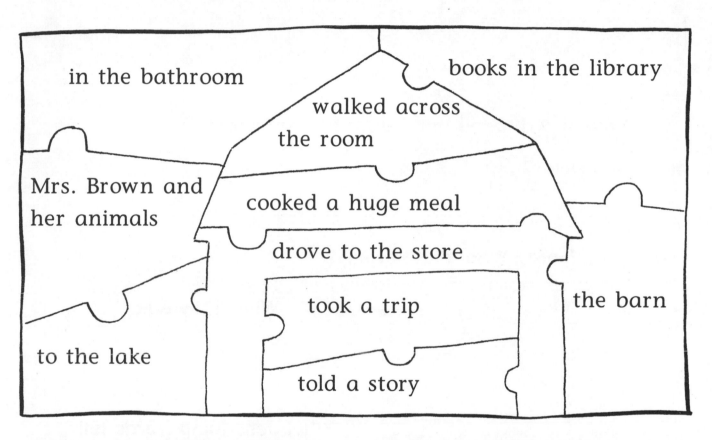

in the bathroom

books in the library

walked across the room

Mrs. Brown and her animals

cooked a huge meal

drove to the store

took a trip

the barn

to the lake

told a story

Now write complete sentences for the puzzle parts that you colored red.

1. _____

2. _____

3. _____

4. _____

5. _____

Organizing a Journal Entry

What is the date of the journal entry?

What happened to me that I want to write about?

Who was there? What did they say?

Who	⟶	What They Said

What happened?

What describing words tell about the events?

Events	⟶	Describing Words

Name _____

Story Time

Use the phrases in the box to complete the sentences.

grabbed her feet   Mrs. Brown's house   in the barn out back

crashed through the floor   to be good   go to the hospital

Saturday: Mrs. Brown rode away on her bicycle. As she went

down the road, a dog _____. Mrs. Brown

got hurt. She had to _____.

Monday: Mrs. Brown sent a letter. She told the animals

_____. But the cow, pigs, ducks, and yak

did not listen. They moved into _____.

Tuesday: When Mrs. Brown came home, she went to bed. She

did not know that the cow, pigs, ducks, and yak were in her

bed. Suddenly, the bed _____. They

all went to the hospital. Soon it was time to go home. Now

they all live together _____.

Name _____

Predicting Outcomes

Read the story and then complete the chart on the next page.

Pets in a Classroom

Mr. Clark's class was excited today. The children had brought their pets to school. There were three little dogs, one puppy, two cats, two kittens, one parrot, two goldfish, one lizard, one snake, two hamsters, one turtle, one rabbit, and even one chicken. The animals sat quietly while Mr. Clark talked about each of them.

At lunchtime the children left the animals in the classroom. As soon as the door was closed, the animals got into trouble. The dogs chased the cats. The hamsters and turtle ate the children's work. The puppy tried to catch the parrot, and the kittens tried to catch the fish. The rabbit knocked over some paint, and it spilled onto the lizard. The snake crawled into Mr. Clark's desk, and the chicken laid an egg on top of it!

When the class got back from lunch, the children saw the mess. But Mr. Clark did not notice.

Name _____

Predicting Outcomes continued

After you read the story, complete the chart below.

What happens in the story?

1. _____

2. _____

3. _____

4. _____

What would happen if . . . ? _____

_____

Tell what happens. _____

_____

What would happen if . . . ? _____

_____

Tell what happens. _____

_____

Name _____

Spelling Spree

Unscramble the letters in each Spelling Word.
Write the word on the line.

1. elin _____

2. ahve _____

3. ltae _____

4. eta _____

5. sdei _____

6. maes _____

7. dame _____

8. idhe _____

9. vige _____

10. zies _____

11. nfie _____

12. iteb _____

1. bite
2. late
3. size
4. made
5. side
6. ate
7. fine
8. same
9. hide
10. line
11. give*
12. have*

Word Meanings

**Read the two meanings for each word. Then write
a sentence for each meaning. The first one has been
done for you.**

Example: land

> The **land** is the ground.
>
> To **land** is to come down.

The farmer's land is flat.
_____

We watch the plane land.
_____

back

> The **back** is the rear part of the body.
> To come **back** is to return.

1. _____

2. _____

tire

> A **tire** is a circle of rubber.
> To **tire** is to get sleepy.

3. _____

4. _____

Vowel Sound Bubbles

Read each word aloud. Listen for the vowel sound.

**Color bubbles that have words with a
short *o* sound yellow.**

**Color bubbles that have words with a
short *u* sound blue.**

**Color bubbles that have words with a
short *e* sound green.**

went

dusting

ducks

frog

just

ten

tested

drops

hospital

butter

Name _____

Proofreading and Writing

Proofreading Find and circle four Spelling Words that are spelled wrong in this puppet show. Write each word correctly.

Mouse: I made a cake for Beth.

Duck: Great! We can givve it to her when she gets home.

Mouse: Look at the cake! Someone took a bitt out of this side.

Duck: It looks fien to me.

Mouse: Maybe I should cut that piece off and make the cake a smaller siz.

Duck: I have a better idea. Let's eat this cake and make a new one for Beth.

Spelling Words

1. bite
2. late
3. size
4. made
5. side
6. ate
7. fine
8. same
9. hide
10. line
11. give*
12. have*

_____   _____

_____   _____

Write an Opinion Write a few sentences telling what you think happened to the cake. Use another sheet of paper. Use Spelling Words from your list.

Theme 1: **Silly Stories** 73

Animal Actions

Complete each sentence to tell what the animals are doing.

Be sure to put a period at the end of each sentence.

> purrs as it naps under a tree   barks at the ducks
>
> trot across the field to the barn   quack loudly
>
> hops on the lily pads in the pond

1. Some horses _____

   _____

2. The ducks in the pond _____

   _____

3. The frog _____

   _____

4. A big brown dog _____

   _____

5. The cat _____

   _____

Goldilocks's Journal

After Goldilocks visited the three bears, she wrote
this plan for a journal entry. On a separate sheet
of paper, write your own journal entry. Use
this plan to help you.

Date

What do I want to write about?

Who was there?   What did they say?

Who ⟶ What They Said

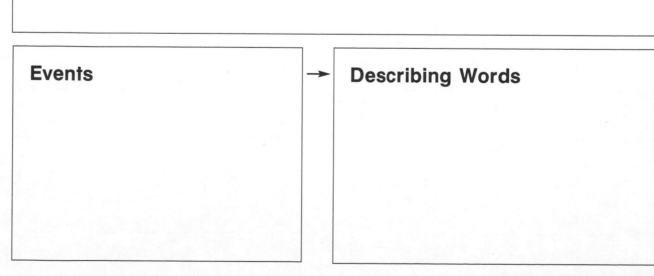

Events ⟶ Describing Words

Listing Actions

The animals did many things while Mrs. Brown was gone. Do the word groups below tell what the animals did? Circle *Yes* or *No*.

1. All the animals.   Yes   No

2. The yak and cow.   Yes   No

3. The ducks rang the doorbell   Yes   No
   many times.

4. The pigs painted the house.   Yes   No

5. One duck.   Yes   No

Add an action part to each word group that does not have one. Write the complete sentences below.

_____

_____

_____

_____

_____

Feeling Words

Write each word from the box next to its meaning.

Vocabulary

cross   observed   thoroughly   unmoved   wicked

1. very mad _____

2. not changed in feelings _____

3. saw _____

4. completely _____

5. very bad _____

**Use the words in sentences. You can use more
than one word in each sentence.**

6. _____

_____

7. _____

_____

8. _____

_____

Name _____

Venn Diagram

**Tell how George and Martha and the hippos in *Hippos*
are alike. Tell how they are different.**

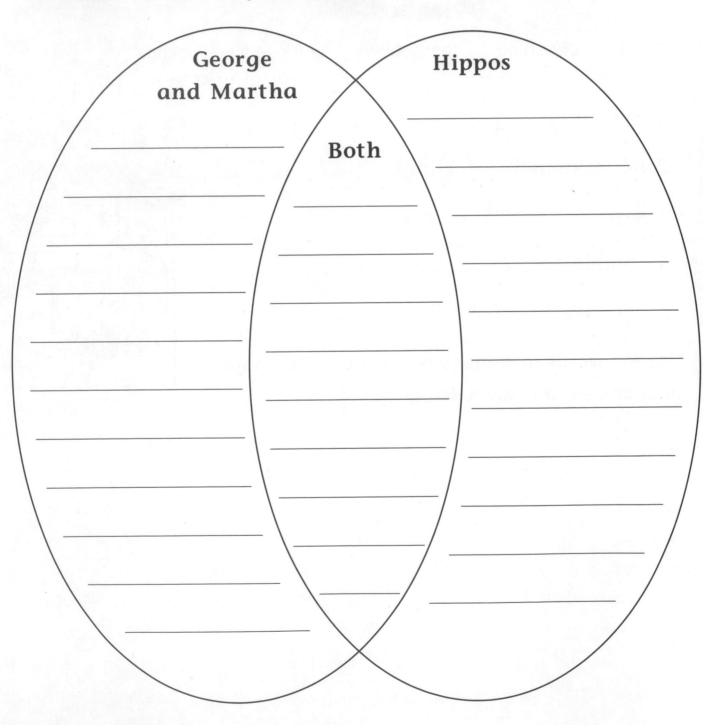

Story Map

Use details from *The Surprise* and *Julius* to fill in the
chart below.

Title	The Surprise	Julius
Who	_____	_____
Where	_____ _____	_____ _____
Beginning	_____ _____ _____	_____ _____ _____
Middle	_____ _____ _____	_____ _____ _____
End	_____ _____ _____	_____ _____ _____

Name _____

Animal Words

Use words from the box to complete the sentences.

.... **Vocabulary** ....

mammal   herds   relatives   nostrils   moisture

1. A bison is a _____, just like a hippo.

2. Bison are _____ of cows.

3. These furry animals move in large _____.

4. Bison have big _____ on their noses.

5. Does a bison's thick fur keep

   _____ away

   from its skin when it rains?

Write three sentences about another mammal.
Use one word from the box in each sentence.

6. _____

7. _____

8. _____

Name _____

Animals

**Write a word from the Word Bank that completes
each sentence.**

Word Bank

| elephant | husky | kitten | otter | rabbit |

1. A _____ is a baby cat.

2. An _____ has a trunk.

3. One kind of big dog is called a _____.

4. A _____ hid in the grass.

5. An _____ swims and plays.

**Say the name of each picture. Write an animal name
that has the same vowel sound.**

_____   _____   _____

Is It a Sentence?

**Write *yes* or *no* to tell whether each of these is
a sentence.**

1. Martha read a funny story.   _____

2. Mad at George.   _____

3. She would not speak to him.   _____

4. Read a joke in a book.   _____

5. A very funny joke.   _____

6. She saw a leaf.   _____

7. It fell down to the ground.   _____

8. Went to George's house.   _____

Write two sentences. Tell about George and Martha.

9. _____

_____

10. _____

_____

Name _____

Spelling Review

Write Spelling Words from the list to answer the questions.

1–14. Which words have the short **a**, **e**, **i**, **o**, or **u** sound?

1. _____   8. _____

2. _____   9. _____

3. _____   10. _____

4. _____   11. _____

5. _____   12. _____

6. _____   13. _____

7. _____   14. _____

15–20. Which words have the long **a** or long **i** sound?

15. _____   18. _____

16. _____   19. _____

17. _____   20. _____

Spelling Words

1. am
2. hide
3. made
4. his
5. nut
6. dig
7. job
8. size
9. fox
10. sat
11. fun
12. late
13. hug
14. wet
15. mop
16. went
17. leg
18. bite
19. ran
20. ate

He Can Do That?

Read the story. Then answer the questions.

Yesterday I left my house late. I ran to the bus stop, but the bus was leaving. I ran after it. I ran faster and faster. Then my feet left the ground. Suddenly, I was flying!

I flew above houses and stores. I passed a robin. It said hello to me!

Finally, I saw my school. I landed on the playground. Then I went into my classroom.

"Hi, Danny," my teacher said. "Why are you here so soon?"

1. What two things in the story are make-believe?

_____

_____

2. What two things in the story are real?

_____

_____

**Think of another make-believe thing that Danny
might do. Write your idea.**

_____

Name _____

Thank You!

Read the letter. Write a word from the box that can be used in place of each underlined word.

Vocabulary

gift   smile   wonderful   happy   receive

October 10, 2004

Dear Sue,

I was so <u>glad</u> that you came to my birthday party! Thank you for the birthday <u>present</u>. It was just what I wanted to <u>get</u>!

What a <u>good</u> time we had that day. It makes me <u>grin</u> to remember it.

Hope to see you soon!

Your friend,
Laura

1. _____   4. _____

2. _____   5. _____

3. _____

Spelling Spree

Silly Scramble Change the order of letters in the words below to make Spelling Words.

Spelling Words

1. tale _____

2. eat _____

3. gel _____

4. dame _____

Spelling Words
1. went
2. bite
3. ran
4. fox
5. made
6. ate
7. nut
8. late
9. leg
10. fun

Rhyme Time Finish the sentences. Write a Spelling Word that rhymes with the word in dark print.

5. Mom and I _____ to buy a new **tent**.

6. I saw a _____ peek out of the **box**.

7. A hungry bird took a _____ from my **kite**.

8. Jason _____ to get a **pan**.

9. Just for _____, let's draw a red **sun**!

10. I found a _____ inside of a **hut**.

Name _____

Writing Naming Parts of Sentences

Read each sentence. Find a naming part in the Word Bank to complete it. Write the word on the line.

Word Bank

sun	fly	fish	leaf	frogs

1. A big _____ flew in the air.

2. Two _____ sat on a lily pad.

3. A little _____ swam in the water.

4. The _____ shone in the sky.

5. A red _____ dropped into the pond.

Name _____

Proofreading and Writing

Proofreading Circle four Spelling Words below that are wrong. Then write them correctly.

I yam a squirrel named Sam. I like to play with my friend Tree. I give her a big hugg each day. We have lots of fun. I hied in her branches. She always finds me! When it is wett, she keeps me dry.

1. _____   3. _____

2. _____   4. _____

Finish the Story Write Spelling Words to complete the sentences in this story.

Sam the squirrel 5. _____ in Tree. He ate 6. _____ last nut. He would have to 7. _____ up more later. Today's 8. _____ was to clean up under Tree. "Tree," Sam asked, "where is the 9. _____ ?"

"You can't use that!" Tree said. "You're too small in 10. _____ .

Finish the Story On another sheet of paper, write a letter from Tree. Use the Spelling Review words.

Name _____

Test Practice

Read each question about *Hippos*. Use the three steps you've learned to choose the best answer. Fill in the circle beside the best answer you chose.

1. Why did the author write *Hippos*?

   ○ to tell a funny story about hippos

   ○ to give interesting facts about hippos

   ○ to make readers want to visit hippos at the zoo

2. What is one way that hippos are like pigs?

   ○ Both like to cover themselves in mud.

   ○ Both are almost as large as rhinos.

   ○ Both can be found in barnyards.

3. **Connecting/Comparing** How is **Mrs. Brown Went to Town** different from **Hippos?**

   ○ **Mrs. Brown Went to Town** is about animals.

   ○ **Mrs. Brown Went to Town** has pictures.

   ○ **Mrs. Brown Went to Town** is a made-up story.

Continue on page 90.

Name _____

Test Practice continued

4. How are hippos like horses?

   ○ Both live in herds and eat grass.

   ○ Both are related to pigs.

   ○ Both like to trot underwater.

5. Why do hippos cover themselves in mud in dry weather?

   ○ to hide themselves

   ○ to keep their skin wet

   ○ to help themselves sleep

6. **Connecting/Comparing** Martha did not like it when George sprayed her with the water hose. How would a real hippo feel if George sprayed it on a hot, sunny day?

   ○ angry

   ○ happy

   ○ dirty

Name _____

Rhyme Time

Write a word from the box to complete each rhyme.

Word Bank

| tadpole | prize | mask | umbrella | mistake |

1. Lion: It's going to rain. Hold an _____ over my mane!

2. Deer: The race was fun. I got first _____. Now I must run!

3. Tiger: Don't make a _____. My stripes are not fake!

4. Raccoon: My _____ helps me hide when I play outside.

5. Frog: I was a _____ when I was young. Growing legs was lots of fun!

Write your own rhyme. Use at least one word with a long vowel and one word with a short vowel.

_____

_____

What Would Happen If . . . ?

**What would happen if the story characters met one
another? Complete the chart.**

What would happen if . . . ?	Tell what happens.
1. Julius sees Martha holding a hose.	
2. George meets Dragon when Dragon wants to get food into his car.	
3. George and Martha visit Julius when he is playing music.	
4. Dragon moves in with Mrs. Brown and the animals.	

Name _____

Add a Vowel

Look at each picture and the word below it. Say the
word. Write the vowel that completes the word.

p ____ nts

s ____ cks

b ____ lt

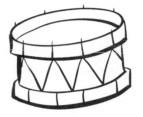
dr ____ m

f ____ sh

c ____ mel

p ____ ncil

b ____ sket

z ____ pper

st ____ plight

b ____ tterfly

b ____ tton

Name _____

Two-Syllable Words

Write each word. Label the vowels and the consonants between them. Divide the word into syllables. Then read the word.

Example: picnic   p i c / n i c
                              v c / c v

1. princess _____   4. cactus _____

2. plastic _____   5. muffin _____

3. dentist _____   6. magnet _____

Answer the clues. Use words from above.

7. It is something to eat. _____

8. It grows where it is hot and dry. _____

9. It can pick up nails. _____

10. Her father is a king. _____

11. Toys are made from it. _____

12. He or she fixes teeth. _____

Name _____

Finish the Rhyme

Write a word from the box that rhymes with each word in dark print. Read each two-line rhyme.

Word Bank

long	know	wall	fly	right	some

1. If the baby bird will **try**,

   Soon it will be able to _____.

2. With gifts I **come**,

   I'll give you _____.

3. The moon and stars light the **night**.

   Do you agree that I'm _____?

4. I took the bat and hit the **ball**,

   It sailed up and over the _____.

5. Do crows walk in the **snow**?

   Is that something you _____?

6. I will sing a **song**.

   It will not take _____.

On another paper, write a sentence for *morning*, *climb*, *want* **and** *thought.*

Name _____

Poetry Words

Circle the word that best completes each sentence.

1. The number of beats in poetry is called the _____.

    rhythm   rhyme   stanza

2. Words with the same ending sounds are words that _____.

    imagine   rhyme   rhythm

3. A group of sentences or lines in a poem is a _____.

    rhythm   stanza   describe

4. Poems usually _____ things, such as feelings or places.

    stanza   rhyme   describe

5. A good poem can help you _____ what it is talking about.

    describe   rhythm   imagine

On another sheet of paper, write three sentences telling what you like or don't like about poetry. Use one of the words you circled in each sentence.

Name _____

Poetry Chart

Fill in the chart.

This poem has rhyming words.
Title _____
Rhyming Words _____
This poem is a shape poem.
Title _____
What is the shape? Who makes the shape? How?
_____
_____
This poem has words I like.
Title _____
Words I like _____
_____
This is a poem I like.
Title _____
Why I like this poem: _____
_____

Comparing Poems

Use the chart below to compare four poems.

Poem	Describes	Makes Me Feel	Rhyming or Unusual Words
Covers			
Why Is It?			
There was a camel			
I Like It When It's Mizzly			

On another paper, draw a picture to go with one of the poems. Write the line or lines from the poem that tell about the picture.

Name _____

Planning a Poem

Fill in the chart.

Topic _____

Picture of Topic

Six Words That Describe the Topic

How It Looks
How It Sounds
How It Feels
How It Tastes
How It Smells

Name _____

Short or Long Sound?

► A single vowel in the middle of a word
often has the short vowel sound.
► The first vowel in a word ending in *e*
often has the long vowel sound.

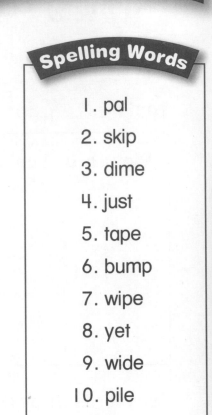

Spelling Words

1. pal
2. skip
3. dime
4. just
5. tape
6. bump
7. wipe
8. yet
9. wide
10. pile

**Write each Spelling Word under the correct
vowel sound.**

Short Vowel Sounds   Long Vowel Sounds

_____   _____

_____   _____

_____   _____

_____   _____

_____   _____

**Write two Spelling Words with the same
vowel sound as *bus*.**

_____   _____

**Write two Spelling Words with the same
vowel sound as *kite*.**

_____   _____

Run-on Sentences

► Correct a run-on sentence by writing it as two sentences.
► Each sentence should have a naming part and an action part.

Write two sentences for each run-on sentence. Add an end mark and capital letter.

1. The gecko is a small lizard it eats insects.

   _____

2. Geckos run around at night some geckos can walk upside down.

   _____

   _____

3. Geckos climb trees they cling to the bark with their toe pads.

   _____

   _____

4. Some geckos make a loud call the female gecko lays two eggs at a time.

   _____

   _____

Name _____

Poetry Chart

Fill in the chart.

This poem has rhyming words.

Title _____

Rhyming Words _____

_____

My own shape poem would be about

_____.

My shape would look like this.

This poem has words I like.

Title _____

Words I like _____

_____

This is a poem I like.

Title _____

Why I like this poem: _____

_____

Name _____

Spelling Spree

Write the Spelling Word for each picture.

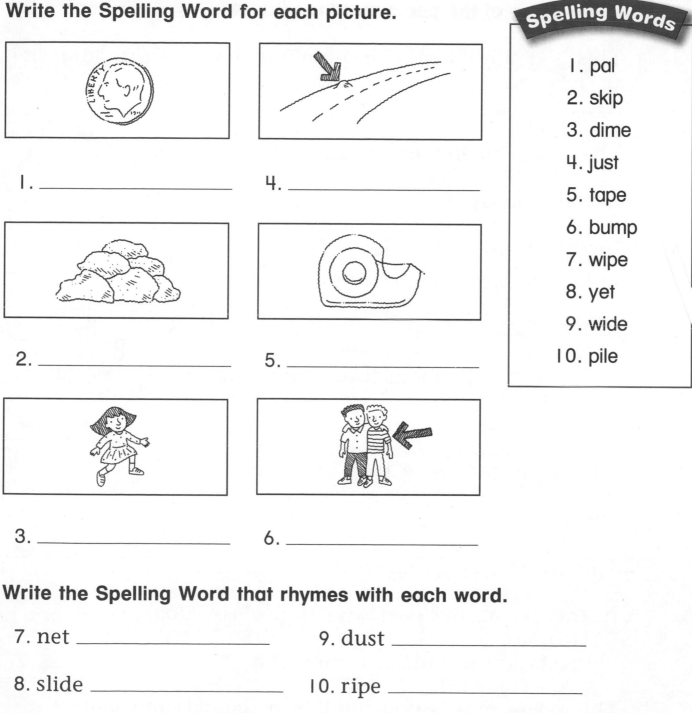

Spelling Words

1. pal
2. skip
3. dime
4. just
5. tape
6. bump
7. wipe
8. yet
9. wide
10. pile

1. _____

2. _____

3. _____

4. _____

5. _____

6. _____

Write the Spelling Word that rhymes with each word.

7. net _____

8. slide _____

9. dust _____

10. ripe _____

Name _____

Poem Clues

Write the name of the poem that fits each clue.

1. This is a silly poem. An animal is down in the dumps!

   _____

2. The words in this poem tell that an animal

   moves quickly. _____

3. In this poem, falling leaves are said
   to be like birds flying south.

   _____

4. This poem tells about those who make

   you feel happy. _____

5. This poem tells why trees seem to

   whisper. _____

6. This poem has sound words. _____

7. In this poem, the poet says that glass, clouds, and

   blankets are all alike in some way. _____

8. This poem makes you think of a foggy, rainy day.

   _____

Name _____

Name That Beat!

Read the lines from two poems. Write the number of beats in each line.

Hint: A word with one syllable has one beat.
Words with two syllables have two beats.

1. There once were two hippos, _____

Who did not smile. _____

2. I like it when it's breezy. _____

It makes me feel so sneezy. _____

Read the first line of each poem below. Finish the next line to make it have the same number of beats. Read the lines to a partner, and clap the beats.

3. There once was a cow with a flute,

Who liked to be _____ and cute.

4. Two ladybugs sit on the sack,

With wings so _____ and spots of _____.

5. I like dogs and cats.

_____

Name _____

Sound Words

Write a sound word from the box to name the sound each animal or thing makes.

Word Bank

pop	squeak	splash	buzz
hoot	hiss	caw	crash

1. bumble bees _____

2. an owl at night _____

3. an angry snake _____

4. thunder _____

5. a balloon breaking _____

6. a crow calling _____

7. a frog jumping in a pond _____

8. a little mouse _____

Write your own sentence using any sound word.
Underline the sound word.

_____

_____

Name _____

Picturing VCCV Words

**Each word below has a VCCV pattern. Draw a line
between the syllables. Read the word. Draw its picture
in the box.**

Example: k i t / t e n

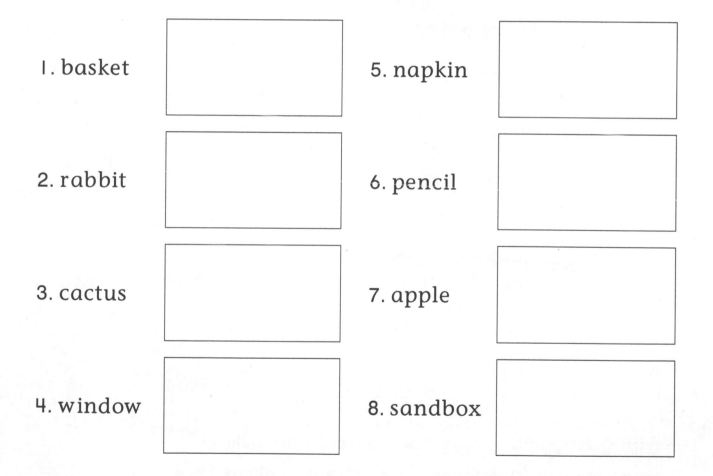

1. basket

2. rabbit

3. cactus

4. window

5. napkin

6. pencil

7. apple

8. sandbox

Read the sentences. Circle words with a VCCV pattern.

9. We had pudding with dinner today.

10. We like to go on picnics in summer.

Name _____

Proofreading and Writing

Proofreading Circle the four Spelling Words that
are spelled wrong. Write each word correctly.

At the Lake

My pol and I swim and splash,

We catch little fish in a net.

And when it is nice and hot,

We ask "Is it time for ice cream yete?

We make a big pil of sand,

Then into the water we run.

We could stay at the lake all day

We are juste having so much fun.

1. pal
2. skip
3. dime
4. just
5. tape
6. bump
7. wipe
8. yet
9. wide
10. pile

1. _____   3. _____

2. _____   4. _____

Writing Rhymes On another paper, write silly
sentences with rhyming words. Use a Spelling
Word and a word that rhymes with it in each
sentence.

Name _____

Fix Run-on Sentences

**Write two sentences for each run-on sentence.
Add an end mark and capital letter.**

1. Your class read a poem about a camel this
   camel has two humps. _____

   _____

2. Camels take people across deserts the deserts
   are hot and dry. _____

   _____

3. A camel goes days without water, it travels
   over hot sands. _____

   _____

4. A camel has long, strong legs it can stand
   seven feet tall. _____

   _____

5. People in Africa use camels to carry things
   you can see camels in zoos. _____

   _____

Name _____

An E-mail Message

1–4. Proofread this e-mail message. Circle two places where periods are missing. Circle two words that need capital letters to begin sentences.

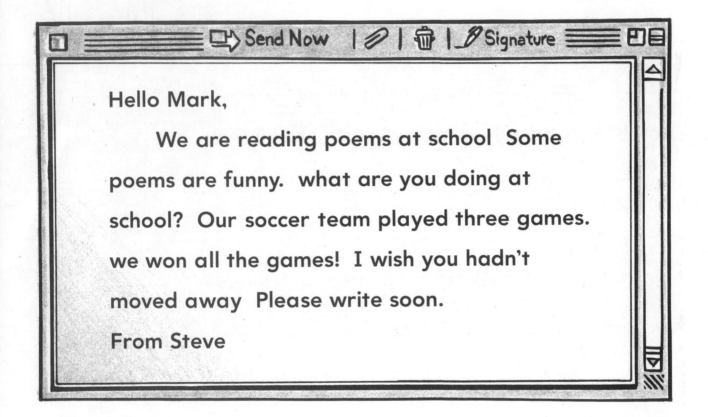

Hello Mark,

    We are reading poems at school Some poems are funny. what are you doing at school? Our soccer team played three games. we won all the games! I wish you hadn't moved away Please write soon.

From Steve

Write each sentence with a mistake correctly.

5. _____

6. _____

7. _____

8. _____

Name _____

Nature Walk

What about nature and the outdoors do you enjoy most?
Describe an event or activity that you have seen or enjoyed
doing outdoors.

_____

_____

_____

_____

_____

_____

_____

Complete the word web with words and phrases that describe a
nature walk you have taken.

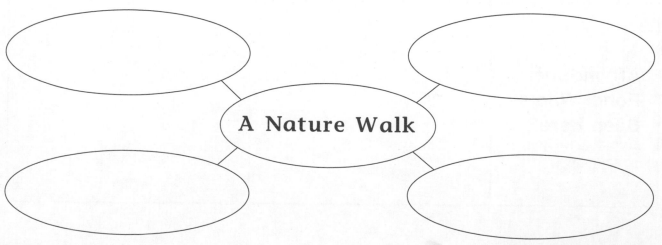

Name _____

Nature Walk

Fill in the chart as you read the stories.

	Where does the nature walk in the story take place?	What do some of the characters see and learn about on their nature walk?
Henry and Mudge and the Starry Night		
Exploring Parks with Ranger Dockett		
Around the Pond: Who's Been Here?		

Name _____

Go Long

Say the name of each picture. Circle the picture of the
word that has the long vowel sound and a silent *e* at the end.

cub   cube

Complete each pair of sentences using the words
in the boxes.

1. My _____ is part of my face.

   My teacher wrote me a _____.

nose   note

2. It is not polite to be _____ to
   other people.
   Follow every school _____.

rule   rude

3. My brother's name is _____.

   _____are my socks.

These   Pete

4. The flag is on the _____.

   Byron told a funny _____.

pole   joke

5. The store is _____.

   Are you _____ today?

closing voting

Tiger and Giraffe Sounds

There are two sounds for the letter **g**. It can

sound like the **g** in the middle of  ,

or it can sound like the **g** at the beginning of

.

Word Bank

gift	gym	huge	page	village
pig	flag	gave	giant	wagon

**Write each word from the box under the word that has
the matching _g_ sound.**

Tiger   **Giraffe**

1. _____   6. _____

2. _____   7. _____

3. _____   8. _____

4. _____   9. _____

5. _____   10. _____

Name _____

Nature Walk

Fill in the chart as you read the stories.

	Where does the nature walk in the story take place?	What do some of the characters see and learn about on their nature walk?
Henry and Mudge and the Starry Night		
Exploring Parks with Ranger Dockett		
Around the Pond: Who's Been Here?		

Name _____

Nature Walk

What about nature and the outdoors do you enjoy most?
Describe an event or activity that you have seen or enjoyed
doing outdoors.

_____

_____

_____

_____

_____

_____

Complete the word web with words and phrases that describe a
nature walk you have taken.

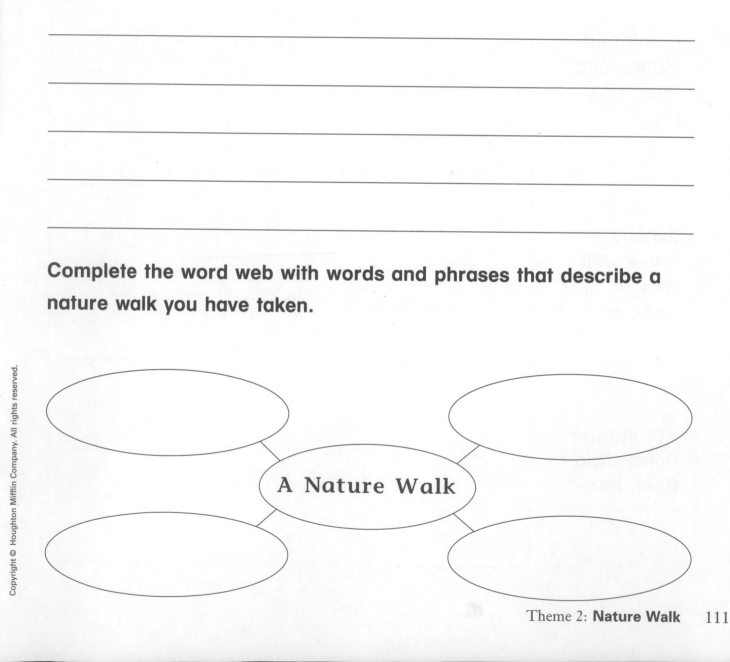

A Nature Walk

Name _____

Tiger and Giraffe Sounds

There are two sounds for the letter **g**. It can

sound like the **g** in the middle of 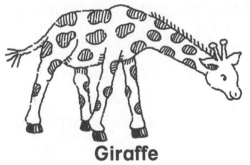 ,

or it can sound like the **g** at the beginning of

 .

Word Bank

gift	gym	huge	page	village
pig	flag	gave	giant	wagon

Write each word from the box under the word that has the matching *g* sound.

Tiger   **Giraffe**

1. _____   6. _____

2. _____   7. _____

3. _____   8. _____

4. _____   9. _____

5. _____   10. _____

Name _____

Puzzle Play

Fill in the puzzle with words from the box that fit the clues.

Word Bank

quiet	even	straight	beautiful	year

Across

1. Last _____ we went camping at Star Lake.
2. It is so _____ there.
3. At night it is very _____.

Down

4. You cannot _____ hear a bird chirping.
5. As soon as it gets dark I go _____ to sleep!

Think of a quiet and beautiful place. Write a sentence about it.

6. _____

_____

_____

Name _____

Camping Words

Use words from the box to label the pictures.

Vocabulary

backpack

lanterns

hike

campfire

tent

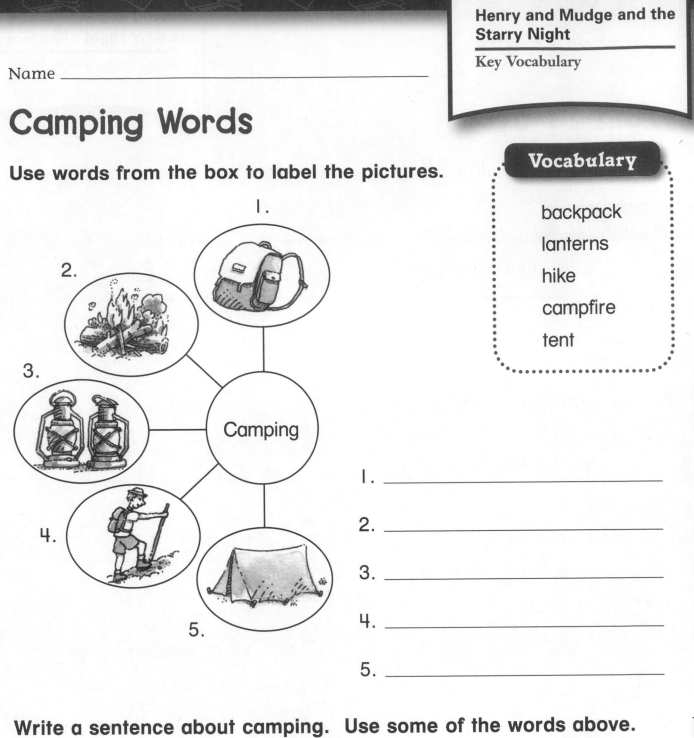

1. _____

2. _____

3. _____

4. _____

5. _____

Write a sentence about camping. Use some of the words above.

6. _____

_____

_____

Name _____

Graphic Organizer

Venn Diagram As you read the story, write what Henry's mother is like, what Henry's father is like, and how both are the same.

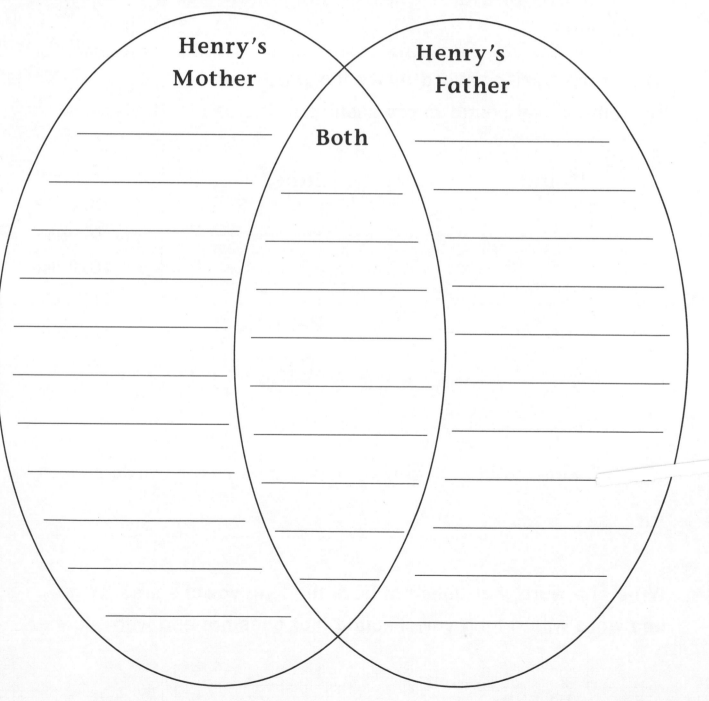

Name _____

Match the Sound

Most of the Spelling Words have the long vowel sound and end with silent *e*.

► The words **one** and **goes** do not follow this rule.

Write each Spelling Word under the word with the same vowel sound and a silent *e* at the end.

1. bone
2. robe
3. use
4. these
5. rope
6. note
7. cute
8. close
9. hope
10. those
11. one*
12. goes*

Home

_____

_____

_____

_____

_____

_____

Cube

_____

_____

Pete

_____

Write one word that does not have the long vowel sound. Write one word with a long vowel sound that does not end with silent *e*.

_____   _____

Sentence or Question?

▶ A telling sentence tells about someone or something. It begins with a capital letter and ends with a period.

▶ A question asks about someone or something. It begins with a capital letter and ends with a question mark.

Unscramble the words to make a telling sentence or a question.

Remember to use capital letters and the correct end marks.

1. fun is camping _____

_____

2. sleep a we in tent _____

_____

3. like you go camping to do _____

_____

Write a telling sentence about the picture.

4. _____

_____

Write a question about the picture.

5. _____

_____

Questions and Answers

Write an answer to each question. Remember to write complete sentences.

BIG BEAR LAKE

BIG RACCOON LAKE

1. **Question:** Where did Henry and his family go camping?

   Answer: _____

   _____

2. **Question:** What did Mudge carry in his backpack?

   Answer: _____

   _____

3. **Question:** What did Henry's father bring with him?

   Answer: _____

   _____

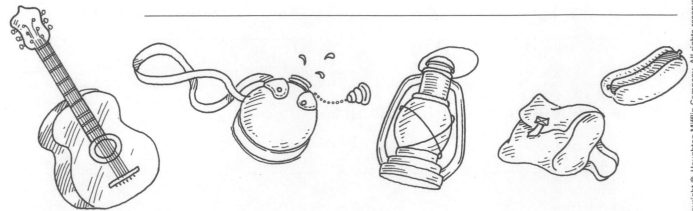

Interviewing Henry

Write the answers Henry might give to these questions.

1. **Question:** Why does your mother know so much about camping?

   Answer: _____

2. **Question:** How did Mudge know you had a cookie in your back pocket?

   Answer: _____

3. **Question:** How did you cook your food?

   Answer: _____

4. **Question:** What did your mother see in the night sky?

   Answer: _____

5. **Question:** Why did you and your family have "green" dreams while camping?

   Answer: _____

   _____

Name _____

Compare and Contrast

Read the story. Complete the diagram on page 123.

Alike and Different

Lori and her parents like the outdoors. One sunny Saturday, the family decided to go hiking at a nearby park. They dressed in their hiking clothes and got their backpacks. Mom put food in her backpack. She told Lori that they would have a picnic lunch. Dad packed a picnic blanket, the first-aid kit, and the park map in his backpack. Lori put only one thing in her backpack. It was her cat, Sprinkles!

The family walked to the park with Sprinkles peeking out from Lori's backpack. In the park, Mom and Dad waved to other hikers they passed. Dad talked about the plants they saw. He knew a lot about plants. Mom looked over her shoulder to check on Lori and Sprinkles.

After a while, the family stopped to rest. Sprinkles took a nap. Mom pointed to some wild animals she saw. Suddenly, Dad decided to be silly. He pretended to be the animals. He scampered like a squirrel, hopped like a rabbit, and flapped his arms like a bird. Lori and her mom laughed.

Compare and Contrast

(continued)

Think about the story you read. Then fill in the chart to tell how Lori's mother and father are alike and different.

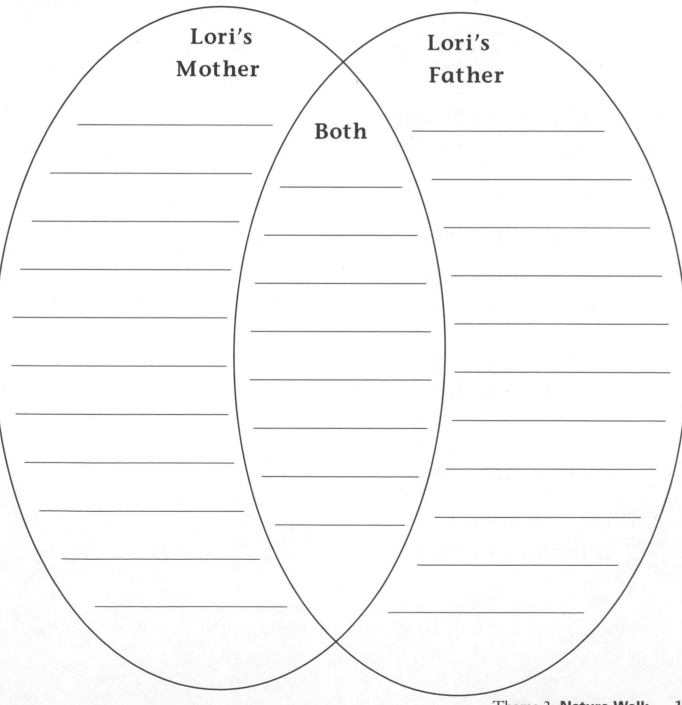

Lori's Mother

Lori's Father

Both

Spelling Spree

Write a Spelling Word for each clue.

1. It rhymes with **flute**.
   It begins like **cup**. _____

2. It rhymes with **toes**.
   It begins like **get**. _____

3. It rhymes with **hose**.
   It begins like **clock**. _____

4. It rhymes with **cone**.
   It begins like **bat**. _____

5. It rhymes with **globe**.
   It begins like **run**. _____

6. It rhymes with **rope**.
   It begins like **home**. _____

7. It rhymes with **vote**.
   It begins like **name**. _____

8. It rhymes with **rose**.
   It begins like **that**. _____

Spelling Words

1. bone
2. robe
3. use
4. these
5. rope
6. note
7. cute
8. close
9. hope
10. those
11. one*
12. goes*

Name _____

One + One = One

A **compound word** is made up of two shorter words. The word **campfire** is a compound word.

Draw a line from the word on the left to the word on the right to make a compound word.

1. sun	storm
2. thunder	rise
3. water	bow
4. rain	fall

Now use each compound word in a sentence.

5. _____

6. _____

7. _____

8. _____

Name _____

Fishing for Vowels

Read the sentences. Draw a circle around each word that has a long vowel sound and that ends with silent *e*.

1. My friend and I live by the lake.
2. We are both nine years old.
3. We are about the same size.
4. I usually sleep late.
5. He comes to wake me up.
6. Then we go fishing and play hide and seek.
7. Sometimes we race our toy cars.
8. My friend is nice.
9. I like him very much.

Now write each word you circled in the fish that has the same vowel sound and a silent *e* at the end.

safe

hide

_____

_____

_____

_____

_____

_____

_____

_____

Proofreading and Writing

Here is a letter Henry might have written. Circle four Spelling Words that are not spelled correctly. Write them correctly on the lines.

Spelling Words

Dear Mom and Dad,

    Thank you for taking Mudge and me camping. The next time we go camping, I'm going to use a stronger rupe on my backpack. The one I did uoos didn't work very well.

    I'm also going to hide wun bone in my roob pocket. I want to see if Mudge can find it like he found the cookie. I hope you like reading this note. Mudge helped me write it.

    Love,

    Henry and Mudge

Henry

Spelling Words

1. bone
2. robe
3. use
4. these
5. rope
6. note
7. cute
8. close
9. hope
10. those
11. one*
12. goes*

_____ _____

_____ _____

Write a Note On another sheet of paper, write a note to someone. Use Spelling Words from the list.

Name _____

Sentence to Question

Read each telling sentence. Turn it into a question. Use words from the box. The first one has been done for you.

Word Bank

Where

Who

When

What

1. Some people love to go camping.

   <u>What do some people love to do?</u>

2. It is fun to go camping in the summer.

   _____

3. My dad likes to sleep in a tent.

   _____

4. I like to go camping at Star Lake.

   _____

What can you do on a camping trip? Write two telling sentences.

5. _____

   _____

   _____

What Do You See?

**Look at the picture. Read the questions and answers.
Rewrite the answers to make them complete sentences.**

1. **Question:** Which animals are sleeping in the cave?
   Answer: the bears

   _____

   _____

2. **Question:** What are the raccoons doing?
   Answer: catching fish

   _____

   _____

3. **Question:** What is the bird doing?
   Answer: sitting in a tree

   _____

   _____

4. **Question:** Which animal is standing under a tree?
   Answer: the deer

   _____

   _____

Name _____

Change It!

**Change these telling sentences to questions.
Remember to begin with a capital letter
and include the correct end mark.**

1. Henry and Mudge went camping in August.

   _____

2. Mudge is Henry's big dog.

   _____

3. Henry's parents took Henry and Mudge camping.

   _____

   _____

**Change these questions into telling sentences. Remember to
begin with a capital letter and include the correct end mark.**

4. Did Mudge have a backpack?

   _____

5. Did Henry want to see a bear?

   _____

   _____

6. Did Henry and his family go hiking?

   _____

Name _____

Revising Your Description

Decide how to make your paper better. Put a check next to the sentences that tell about your writing.

Superstar

☐ I told what I am describing.

☐ I used many details and sensory words. I told about more than one sense.

☐ I wrote the details in a clear order.

☐ My writing shows how I feel.

☐ I wrote complete sentences, and there are few mistakes.

Rising Star

☐ I need to tell what I am describing.

☐ I need more details and sensory words. I should tell about more than one of sense.

☐ I did not write the details in order.

☐ My writing doesn't show how I feel.

☐ Some of my sentences aren't complete. There are many mistakes.

Name _____

Writing Sentences

**Read each group of words. Write the group
of words that is a sentence.**

1. All kinds of people come to the river.
   All kinds of people.

   _____

2. In the river.
   My dad likes to catch fish in the river.

   _____

3. Different birds and bugs.
   I see different birds and bugs here.

   _____

4. Life on the river changes from season to season.
   From season to season.

   _____

**Think of an outdoor spot you enjoy. Write two sentences about it.
Make sure your sentence tells what someone or something is doing.**

5. _____

6. _____

Name _____

Spelling Words

These Spelling Words are words that you use in your writing. Look carefully at how they are spelled. Write the missing letters in the Spelling Words below. Use the words in the box.

1. o____   7. fr____m

2. w_____t   8. d_____s

3. a____   9. h_____

4. h_____   10. th____r____

5. c_____e   11. g_____s

6. ____f   12. the_____

Write the Spelling Words below.

_____   _____

_____   _____

_____   _____

_____   _____

_____   _____

Spelling Words

1. on
2. am
3. come
4. if
5. does
6. goes
7. from
8. his
9. want
10. her
11. their
12. there

Name _____

Spelling Spree

Write a Spelling Word to finish each riddle.

1. I'm made _____ wood.
   You can write with me.

2. I swim _____ in the lake.
   I have scales and fins.

3. I _____ out at night.
   I rhyme with soon.

4. I _____ on a wall.
   You can see yourself in me.

5. I am _____ best friend.
   She likes me.
   I bark and run.

Write the Spelling Word that matches the clue.

6. the opposite of **off**   _____

7. to do something   _____

8. to go somewhere   _____

9. to wish for something   _____

10. shows something belongs
    to some people   _____

Name _____

Proofreading and Writing

Proofreading Find and circle misspelled Spelling Words below. Then write each word correctly.

The little bird landed on the fence post. He had cume from the woods. His feathers were brown with speckles of black. "Ef he is hungry, he will wunt the seeds," I thought.

Suddenly he swooped down onto the deck. He pecked the tiny, hard seeds I had thrown thair. Suddenly, he lifted hiz head as if he heard a sound. He flapped his wings and flew off into the woods.

Spelling Words

1. on
2. am
3. come
4. if
5. does
6. goes
7. from
8. his
9. want
10. her
11. their
12. there

_____ _____

_____ _____

_____

Write and Draw an Animal On another sheet of paper, draw pictures of some animals you might see in your backyard. Write a sentence below each picture that tells about the animal. Use as many Spelling Words as you can.

Name That!

Write the name of each picture. Then circle the
consonant cluster.

Example:

(present)

1. _____

2. _____

3. _____

4. _____

5. _____

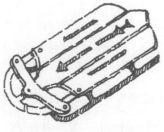

6. _____

7. _____

8. _____

136   Theme 2: **Nature Walk**

Name _____

Camping Trip

Read the story. Circle the words in which the letter *c* makes the same sound you hear at the beginning of the word *sand*.

Juan and Hal went to the park to camp. They were far from the city. They carried their equipment to the pond and set up their tent near a fence. It was a cold night, so they collected wood and made a big fire. Their faces glowed in the firelight. They cooked hot dogs. Then they ate cookies and went to sleep. In the morning there was a thin layer of ice on the pond. But Juan and Hal were warm in their tent!

Now read the story again. Draw a line under the words in which *c* makes the same sound you hear at the beginning of *cup*.

Name _____

A Ranger's Day

Read what one park ranger did at work today.
Circle these words: busy, important, later, touch,
young. Then answer the questions.

10:00 Collect seeds to plant later this week.
12:30 Eat lunch with the other rangers to
stay in touch.
2:00 Check on the young deer at the zoo.
3:00 *Important: Help the class plant trees.
5:00 Go home after this busy day!

1. Why did the park ranger eat lunch with the
other rangers?

_____

_____

2. What animals did he check on?

_____

_____

3. What kind of day did the park ranger have?

_____

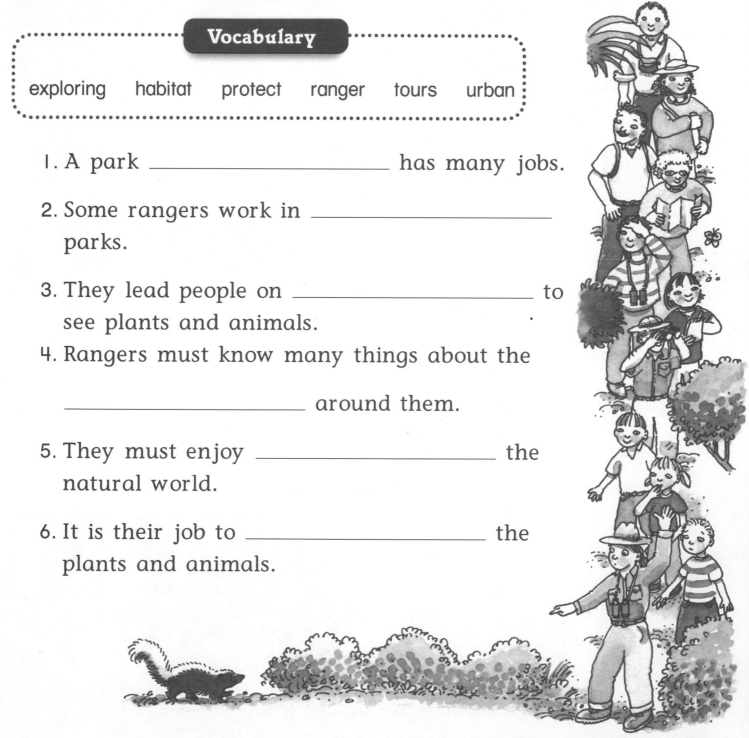

Name _____

A Special Job

Use words from the box to finish the sentences. They will tell about a very special job.

> **Vocabulary**
>
> exploring   habitat   protect   ranger   tours   urban

1. A park _____ has many jobs.

2. Some rangers work in _____ parks.

3. They lead people on _____ to see plants and animals.

4. Rangers must know many things about the _____ around them.

5. They must enjoy _____ the natural world.

6. It is their job to _____ the plants and animals.

Name _____

K-W-L Chart

Complete this chart.

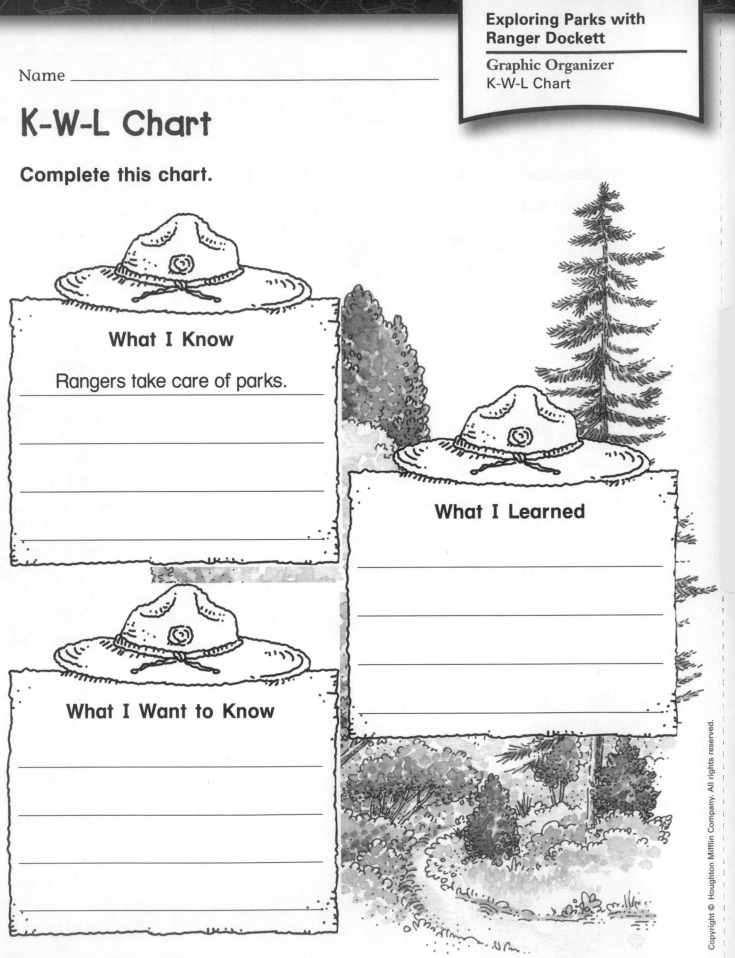

What I Know

Rangers take care of parks.

What I Want to Know

What I Learned

Name _____

Consonant Clusters

A **consonant cluster** is two consonant
letters whose sounds are blended together.
Some consonant clusters are **tr**, **sw**, **st**, **cl**,
xt, **br**, and **gl**.

**Write the Spelling Words that begin with a
consonant cluster.**

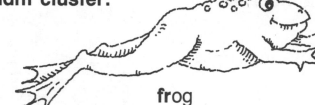

frog

_____   _____

_____   _____

_____   _____

_____

**Write the Spelling Words that end with a
consonant cluster.**

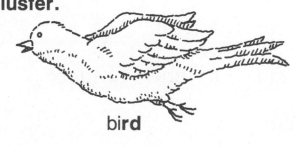

bird

_____   _____

_____

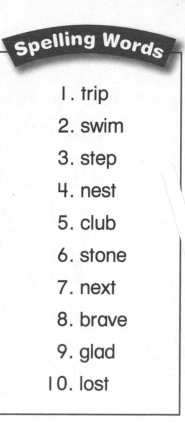

Spelling Words

1. trip
2. swim
3. step
4. nest
5. club
6. stone
7. next
8. brave
9. glad
10. lost

Find the Commands

A command

► is a sentence that tells someone what to do

► has an understood subject **you**

► begins with a capital letter and ends with a period

Read the sentences below. If a sentence is a command, write C on the line next to it.

_____ 1. Who likes to go to the park?

_____ 2. Dogs run in the park.

_____ 3. Keep your dog on a leash.

_____ 4. Don't throw balls near the pond.

_____ 5. The park is always open.

_____ 6. Don't pick the flowers.

_____ 7. Some people like to run in the park.

_____ 8. Keep your bike on the trail.

_____ 9. When can we meet the park ranger?

_____ 10. Use the trash cans.

Choose a Topic

How do you choose a topic to write about?
You can choose a topic you already know about
or want to know about.

Write three topics you already know about.

1. _____

2. _____

3. _____

Choose one of these topics and write it inside the box in the middle. Then write something you know about this topic in each of the other four boxes.

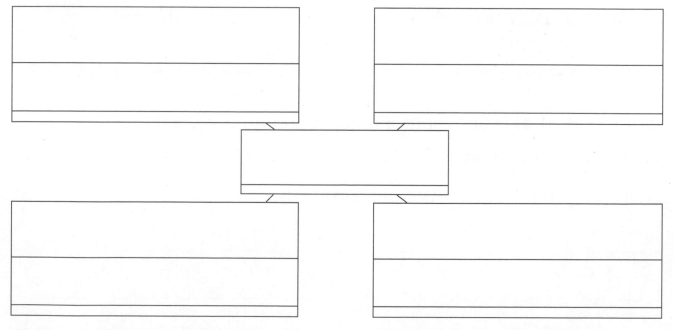

Write a sentence that tells what your paragraph will be about.

_____

Describe the Job

Read the want ad. Write a word to complete each sentence.

Park Ranger Needed!
Central Park needs a new ranger. To do this job well, you must be able to lead people on

_____ of the park. You must keep

in _____ with other rangers. You

must _____ trees, help people follow

the park _____, and teach classes

about the plants and _____ found
in the park.

What kind of person would make a good park ranger? Finish this sentence.

A good park ranger is someone who

_____

_____

_____

_____

Fact and Opinion

Read the story. Answer the questions on page 146.

The Park in Winter

The park is a fun place to go in the winter. When the pond freezes, it is a good place to ice skate. There is a small building by the pond. Inside the building it is nice and warm. You can even buy delicious hot chocolate there.

When it snows, bring your sled. The hill is a good place for sledding. The snow on the hill is soft and deep. Be careful around the trees. You don't want to crash! Sometimes there are twenty children sledding on the hill. They wear hats, gloves, and boots to stay warm. Their sleds are red, green, blue, and yellow. There are so many colors! Sledding is fun for everyone.

Right after the snow falls, the park is very quiet. The snow helps to make it quiet. But if you listen, you might hear a woodpecker pecking an old tree. It is looking for bugs to eat. A busy woodpecker is noisy.

Fact and Opinion (continued)

Think about what you read. Then write facts or opinions from the story.

Write one fact about the building.

_____

Write an opinion about hot chocolate.

_____

Write one fact about the children sledding.

_____

Write an opinion about sledding.

_____

Write one fact about woodpeckers.

_____

Write one opinion about woodpeckers.

_____

What do you like about the park in winter?
Write one fact and one opinion.

Fact: _____

Opinion: _____

Spelling Spree

Combine letters from the two frogs to make the Spelling Words that begin with two consonants.

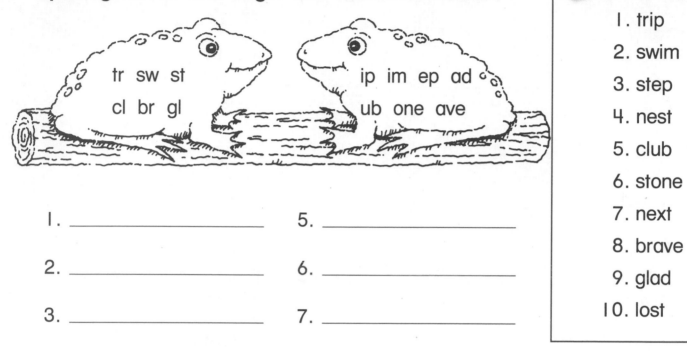

tr sw st
cl br gl

ip im ep ad
ub one ave

1. trip
2. swim
3. step
4. nest
5. club
6. stone
7. next
8. brave
9. glad
10. lost

1. _____
2. _____
3. _____
4. _____

5. _____
6. _____
7. _____

Combine letters from the two birds to make Spelling Words that end with two consonants.

ne lo

st xt

8. _____
9. _____

10. _____

Name _____

Match the Opposites

Draw a line from each word on the left to a word on the right that has the opposite meaning.

1. sad   found

2. lost   finish

3. never   happy

4. thick   thin

5. below   always

6. start   above

Think of words that mean the opposite of each of the words below. Write those words on the lines.

7. front _____   9. dark _____

8. soft _____   10. asleep _____

Vowel Fun

Draw a circle around each word that has a long vowel sound and that ends with silent *e*.

some   home

holes   poke   these

hear   huge   love

went   cute

Use the words you circled to finish these sentences.

1. The park is _____ to many animals.

2. Once I saw a _____ little frog.

3. Some birds live in _____ in the trees.

4. I passed a turtle that started to

   _____ its head out of its shell.

5. A horse was standing next to a

   _____ tree.

6. All _____ animals make the park a fun place.

Proofreading and Writing

Proofreading Read the sentences below. Find
three Spelling Words that are not spelled correctly.
Draw a circle around the words. Then write each
word correctly.

What to do on the class field trip:

1. Look for a nets.

2. Look under a ston for bugs.

3. Find the place where the fish smim.

Spelling Words

1. trip
2. swim
3. step
4. nest
5. club
6. stone
7. next
8. brave
9. glad
10. lost

1. _____

2. _____

3. _____

Writing What kinds of things does a bird do? Write
two sentences about a bird. Use some of your
Spelling Words in your sentences.

_____

_____

_____

Command Some Fun

Read each sentence about the park. Then change it into a command.

1. I want you to have fun in the park.

   _____

2. You can meet the other park rangers at noon.

   _____

3. I think you should listen to the birds.

   _____

4. Everyone can take a picture of the deer.

   _____

5. You should stay on the trail.

   _____

Adding Details

This park ranger needs your help. Add details to his invitation to make it more interesting. The birds show where to add details. Write the new invitation below.

There are many things to see in the park! In the ⬡ pond, there are ⬡ ducks swimming. Many ⬡ mushrooms grow under the ⬡ trees. Squirrels are getting ready for a ⬡ winter. Let me show you around the park.

Come to the park!

_____

_____

_____

_____

_____

_____

Use Good Manners

**Read this note that a park ranger wrote.
Look for places to make it more polite.**

> We are going on a field trip to the pond. Be ready for a big adventure. This trip will be fun. Wear rubber boots or old shoes. Your feet might get wet. Bring a sweater or jacket. The air is cool in the fall. Don't bring any more than you need. But bring a smile!

**Write the note again. Add the word *please* in five places.
Use capital letters and end marks correctly.**

_____

_____

_____

_____

_____

_____

_____

Name _____

A Funny Game

**Answer each pair of clues using
the words from the boxes.**

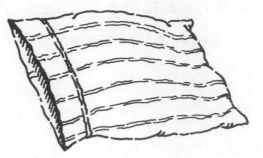

1. You rest your head on it. _____

   Someone who flies a jet _____

   | pilot   pillow |

2. Play time at school _____

   It flies up into the sky. _____

   | recess   rocket |

3. Very quick _____

   You use it on a shirt. _____

   | button   sudden |

4. Twelve eggs _____

   A bird with a red chest _____

   | robin   dozen |

5. Very quiet _____

   A dark place _____

   | silent   tunnel |

Name _____

What a Great Day!

Read the story below. Use the words in the box to finish the story. You will use each word two times.

Word Bank

across	brother	great	stand

My _____ and I went to the

pond. We walked _____ the

bridge. I asked him to _____

next to a tall pine tree. I took his picture. My

_____ looked small next to that

_____ big tree. He could not

_____ still for very long. When

we looked _____ the pond, we

saw our father. He was bringing us lunch. He

gave us some _____ sandwiches.

We had fun together at the pond.

Theme 2: **Nature Walk**   155

Name _____

What's the Word?

Take a trip to the pond. Use words from the box to answer each question.

Word Bank

bank	crater	edge	moss	path	shallow

1. What do you follow to get to the pond?

   _____

2. What do you call the line where the water

   begins or ends? _____

3. What might you see growing under a tree?

   _____

4. What must you climb down to get to the

   pond? _____

5. What is another name for a hole in the

   ground? _____

6. What word describes water that is not

   very deep? _____

Name _____

Around the Pond Chart

As you read the story, complete the chart below by writing other categories of animals that Cammy and William found at the pond.

Birds	
_____ _____ _____	_____ _____ _____
_____ _____ _____	_____ _____ _____

Name _____

Double Consonants

In words like **bell**, **off**, and **dress**, the final consonant sound is spelled with two letters that are the same.

Write the Spelling Words that end with the same double consonant as *ball*.

1. _____

2. _____

3. _____

4. _____

5. _____

Write the Spelling Words that end with the same double consonant as *dress*.

6. _____

7. _____

Write the three Spelling Words that remain.

8. _____

9. _____

10. _____

Excitement at the Pond

► A command is a sentence that tells someone to do something.
► An exclamation is a sentence that shows a strong feeling, such as surprise or fear.

Read each sentence. Write C if it is a command. Write E if it is an exclamation.

____ 1. Ming: I see a muskrat!

____ 2. John: Let's take a picture of it!

____ 3. Ming: Be very quiet.

____ 4. John: Take a picture now.

Write each group of words as a command or an exclamation. Use a capital letter and the correct end mark.

5. don't get close to the pond

_____

6. be careful where you step

_____

7. the water is cold

_____

Name _____

Learning Log

As you read the story, write a learning log entry for one of the pages in the story.

Notes About the Story	My Thoughts About My Notes
_____	_____
_____	_____
_____	_____
_____	_____
_____	_____
_____	_____
_____	_____
_____	_____
_____	_____
_____	_____

Follow the Clues!

Finish the chart. Write either the clues or the names of the animals that Cammy and William found at the pond.

Clue	Animal
1. white feathers stuck to bark	_____
2. _____	raccoon
3. _____	beaver
4. crater on sandy bottom of water	_____
5. _____	garter snake
6. _____	great blue heron
7. pile of mussel shells in mud	_____

Name _____

Categorize and Classify

Read the story below. Complete the chart on page 163.

Around the Swamp

Wanda likes to visit the swamp. A swamp is a place that is very wet. Wanda's dad takes her around the swamp in his boat. They float under willow trees and gum trees.

Many animals live in the swamp. Wanda looks out for cottonmouth snakes. She knows they are very dangerous. Wanda's dad likes to watch for birds. He points out the hawks and vultures in the sky. There are many animals in the swamp that they never see. The fox only comes out at night, and the bobcat stays away from people. There is bass in the water, but the water is too dark to see the fish.

From the boat, Wanda can see turtles. The turtles lie in the sun and hardly move. Once they saw a raccoon catching a fish. But the most exciting day at the swamp was when they saw two black bear cubs running between the trees.

Categorize and Classify
(continued)

After you've read the story, complete the chart below.

At the bottom of the chart, make up your own category about the swamp. Write some examples.

Category	Examples
Trees	
Snake	
Birds	
An Animal That Comes out at Night	
Fish	
An Animal That Eats Fish	

Name _____

Spelling Spree

Write the Spelling Word that answers each riddle.

You can hear me ring.
What am I?

_____

You must clean me up.
What am I?

_____

If you drop me, my shell will break.
What am I?

_____

Climb up me. Roll back down.
What am I?

_____

Water me to keep me green.
What am I?

_____

Use a bucket to get my water.
What am I?

_____

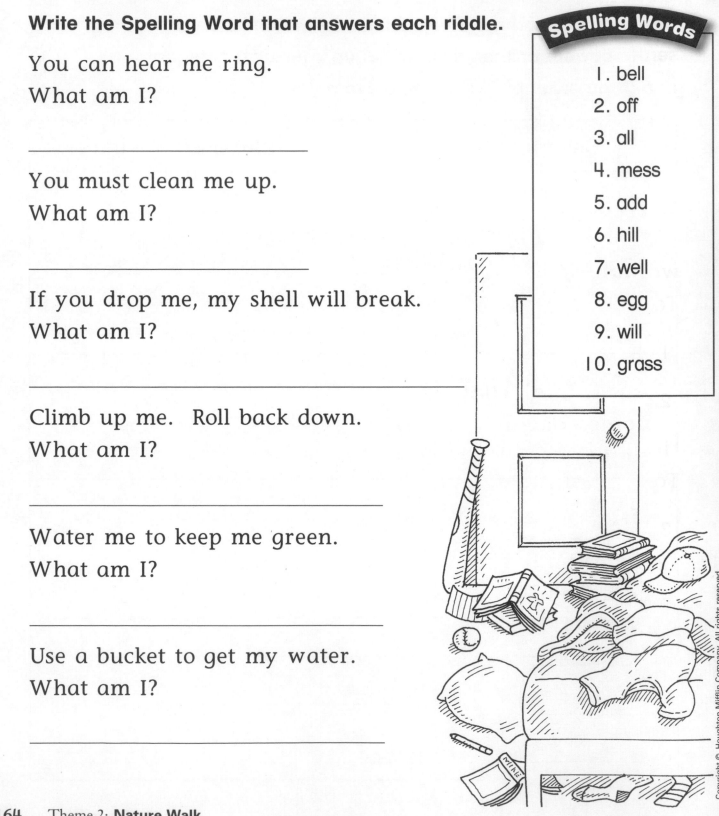

Name _____

What Do You Mean?

**Read the two meanings for each word. Then write a
sentence for each meaning.**

Example: **can**

A **can** is something that soup comes in.

The word **can** means to be able to do something.

I will open the can.

Mary can read hard books.

watch: A **watch** is a small clock worn on the wrist.
To **watch** means to look at something.

1. _____

2. _____

tie: A **tie** is something men wear.
To **tie** means to fasten or close up something.

3. _____

4. _____

bark: **Bark** is what dogs do.
Bark is the covering on a tree.

5. _____

6. _____

Name _____

Blend the Sounds

Word Bank

| trip | stop | planting | fly | dry | sniff |

Write each word in the box under the picture whose
name begins with the same sound. Then write two other
words that begin with the same sound.

1. _____

2. _____

3. _____

4. _____

5. _____

6. _____

7. _____

8. _____

9. _____

10. _____

11. _____

12. _____

13. _____

14. _____

15. _____

16. _____

17. _____

18. _____

Proofreading and Writing

Proofreading Circle four Spelling Words that are spelled wrong. Then write each word correctly.

Dear Grandma,

   Today I walked to the pond with three friends. We alll sang as we walked. We passed some workers. They were deciding on where to ad more paths to the pond. We had fun watching a group of baby birds fly uff. We also saw a tiny blue egg in a nest. Soon a bird wil hatch from it!

                   Love,
                   Maria

Spelling Words

1. bell
2. off
3. all
4. mess
5. add
6. hill
7. well
8. egg
9. will
10. grass

1. _____

2. _____

3. _____

4. _____

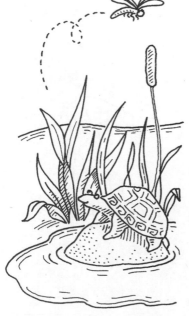

Write a Letter On a separate piece of paper, write a letter to someone in your family. Tell them what you would like to see or do at the pond. Use Spelling Words from the list.

Name _____

Who's at the Pond?

Under each picture write what Jenny is saying. Each
sentence should be an *exclamation*.

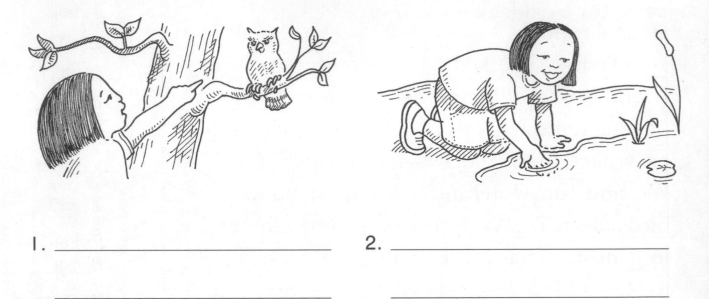

1. _____

_____

2. _____

_____

Pedro is at the pond with his mother. Look at the pictures.
Under each picture write what Pedro's mother says to him.
Each sentence should be a *command*.

3. _____

_____

4. _____

_____

Tell More About the Story

Read the sentences in column A that tell about the story.

In column B, add more details to each sentence. Write your new sentence on the line.

Story: Around the Pond	
A Telling About the Story	**B** Adding More Details
William and Cammy see white feathers.	_____ _____ _____ _____
A tree has fallen.	_____ _____ _____ _____
Cammy saw a shape on the tree.	_____ _____ _____

Name _____

It's a Field Trip!

**Read the announcement for the field trip to the pond.
Each sentence should be an exclamation or a command.
Check the capital letters and end marks for each
sentence. Circle any mistakes.**

We're going on a field trip. plan to be gone
all morning? bring a sweater! bring a snack?
We're ready to have a good time.

**In the space below, write the announcement using
capital letters and end marks correctly.**

_____

_____

_____

_____

_____

_____

Name _____

Word Puzzle

**Read the sentences. Write the words that complete
them in the puzzle.**

Vocabulary

owling   shadows   clearing   echo   meadow   pumped

Across

1. The owl _____ its wings and flew away.

2. The tree's _____ made dark patterns on the snow.

3. There are no trees in the _____ in the woods.

Down

4. I yelled, "Hello!" and
   heard my _____.

5. Flowers and grass
   grow in the _____.

6. We go _____ on
   winter nights.

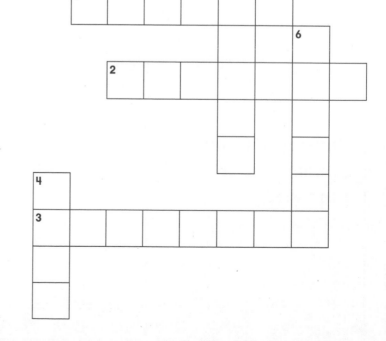

Name _____

Compare Owl Stories

Fill in the chart as you read the stories.

	Owl Moon	Owls
What is the selection about?		
Why did the author write the selection?		
What are some details you enjoyed reading?		

Name _____

What Did They See?

What did the girl in *Owl Moon* see, hear, and feel? How were her experiences the same and different from the children in *Around the Pond: Who's Been Here?* Fill in the chart to tell.

	Owl Moon	Around the Pond: Who's Been Here?
See	_____ _____ _____	_____ _____ _____
Feel	_____ _____ _____	_____ _____ _____
Hear	_____ _____ _____	_____ _____ _____

Name _____

Who Am I?

Complete each clue with a word from the box.
Write a letter on each line.

Vocabulary

swoops   active   outlined   blend   curved

1. My dark colors help me ___ ___ ___ (7) ___

   in with the trees.

2. My eyes are (6) ___ ___ ___ ___ ___ ___

   with black circles, like a mask.

3. I am (2) (3) ___ ___ ___ ___ at night.

4. A bird ___ ___ (5) ___ ___ ___ through the air,

   but I walk on the ground.

5. My tail is straight, not (4) ___ (1) ___ ___ ___

   like a dog's tail.

Now use the circled letters to solve the riddle.

6. I live in the forest and come out at night. What am I?

   I am a ___ ___ ___ ___ ___ ___ ___ .
        1   2   3   4   5   6   7

**Monitoring
Student Progress**

Review Phonics Long Vowels
CVC*e: o, e, u;* Two Sounds
for *g;* Consonant Clusters

Name _____

What Am I?

Write a word to answer each riddle.

Word Bank

smoke	huge	stage	mole
flute	mule	globe	bridge

1. I look like a horse. I'm a

   _____.

2. Cars go on me to get across the

   river. I'm a _____.

3. You play music on me.

   I'm a _____.

4. I'm a round map. I'm a _____.

5. I dig holes in the ground. I'm a _____.

6. I mean "very, very big." I'm _____.

7. If there's a fire in the fireplace, I come out of the

   chimney. I'm _____.

8. You dance and sing on me. I'm a _____.

Theme 2: **Nature Walk**   175

Sentence to Question

Read each telling sentence. Write a question that it answers. Use words from the box.

Word Bank

When	Who	Where	What

1. My sister looks for owls.

   _____

2. I take walks in the woods.

   _____

3. Owls hunt at night.

   _____

4. Those birds eat mice.

   _____

**What animal would you like to see in the woods?
Write two telling sentences.**

5. _____

   _____

Name _____

Spelling Review

Write Spelling Words from the list to answer the questions.

1–7. Which words have the long **a**, **e**, **o**, or **u** sound spelled vowel-consonant-e?

1. _____   5. _____

2. _____   6. _____

3. _____   7. _____

4. _____

8–15. Which words have the consonant cluster **tr**, **sw**, **st**, **cl**, **br**, **gl**, or **xt**?

8. _____   12. _____

9. _____   13. _____

10. _____   14. _____

11. _____   15. _____

16–22. Which words have double consonants?

16. _____   20. _____

17. _____   21. _____

18. _____   22. _____

19. _____

Spelling Words

1. lost
2. these
3. glad
4. grass
5. hope
6. cute
7. trip
8. swim
9. off
10. bone
11. egg
12. next
13. stone
14. mess
15. brave
16. use
17. add
18. club
19. all
20. hill

Theme 2: **Nature Walk**   177

Name _____

Fact and Opinion

Read the paragraphs. Then answer the questions.

Digging for Clams

Clams live under wet sand or mud. A clam's shell has two parts that open and close. The clam opens its shell to get food. A clam with an open shell looks scary!

Some people dig for clams. Digging for clams is not fun. Clams are good to eat, though. You can buy clams at a fish shop.

What are two facts about clams?

1. _____

2. _____

What are two opinions about digging for clams?

3. _____

4. _____

Name _____

Match the Opposites

Read each word. Write an antonym for it on the line.

1. cold   _____

2. over   _____

3. closed   _____

4. fast   _____

5. full   _____

6. shallow   _____

7. begin   _____

8. top   _____

Write a sentence that uses a word and its antonym.

_____

_____

_____

Name _____

Spelling Spree

Double Delights Write the Spelling Word that answers each question.

1. What can you hike up? _____

2. What grows in yards? _____

3. What does a chicken lay? _____

4. What is the opposite of **none**?

_____

Riddles Write a Spelling Word to answer each riddle.

5. This is something a dog likes. What is

   this? _____

6. You do this in the water. What is this? _____

7. This is a group you join. What is this? _____

8. You can use this to build. What is this? _____

9. You can do this with numbers. What is this?

_____

10. If you are happy, you feel this way. What is this?

_____

Spelling Words
1. bone
2. hill
3. egg
4. swim
5. grass
6. all
7. stone
8. glad
9. club
10. add

Name _____

Looking for Commands

Read the sentences below. If a sentence is a command, write C on the line next to it.

_____ 1. Owls fly quietly.

_____ 2. Listen for a hoot.

_____ 3. Hand me the flashlight.

_____ 4. An owl is in the tall tree.

_____ 5. Do you see it yet?

_____ 6. Stay very quiet.

_____ 7. Two eyes are staring at us!

_____ 8. Take a picture now.

Write two of your own commands.

9. _____

_____

10. _____

_____

Name _____

Proofreading and Writing

Proofreading Circle four Spelling Words that are
wrong below. Then write each word correctly.

Dear Gran,

    Yesterday I went on a tripp to the

lake with Mom. We saw cyute fish!

    I have to go clean my room now. It is

a mes! I hoap you will write back soon.

          Love,

          Celia

1. brave
2. lost
3. cute
4. use
5. next
6. mess
7. off
8. these
9. hope
10. trip

1. _____   3. _____

2. _____   4. _____

**Word for Word Write the Spelling Word that means
the opposite of each word or words.**

5. scared _____   7. waste _____   9. on _____

6. found _____   8. before _____   10. those _____

✏️ **Write a Story Write a story about a family on
a nature walk. Write on another sheet of paper.
Use the Spelling Review Words.**

Name _____

Test Practice

Read each sentence about *Owls*. Then choose the answer that best completes each sentence. Use the three steps you learned. Then fill in the circle beside the best answer.

1. Owls use their eyes and ears to _____.

   ○ hunt for food
   ○ turn their necks
   ○ sit on high branches
   ○ clean themselves

2. It is hard to find owls in the woods because they ____.

   ○ live on the ground
   ○ hunt mice and other pests
   ○ sleep in holes
   ○ are the same color as the trees

3. **Connecting/Comparing** In **Owl Moon**, a girl and her father look for owls. In **Owls**, you learned why people go looking for owls ____.

   ○ with hats
   ○ at night
   ○ in the meadow
   ○ in winter

Continue on page 184.
Theme 2: **Nature Walk**   **183**

Name _____

Test Practice continued

4. Owls can surprise mice because _____.

   ○ mice make lots of noise
   ○ owls fly very quietly
   ○ mice cannot run quickly
   ○ owls can see behind themselves

5. The author thinks that owls _____.

   ○ hurt people
   ○ do not see well
   ○ do not hunt well
   ○ help people

6. **Connecting/Comparing** The wood ducks in **Around the Pond** are like owls because they _____.

   ○ live near ponds
   ○ have feathers
   ○ hunt mice
   ○ can see in the dark

Name _____

Long or Short?

**Read each sentence. Draw a line under the two words
in each sentence that have the VCV pattern.**

1. The baby spiders sat on a leaf.

2. Those ants make tiny shadows!

3. Please finish your salad.

4. Does that planet have craters on it?

**Read each word you underlined. If the first syllable has
a long vowel sound, write the word under *tiger*. If the
first syllable has a short vowel sound, write the word
under *camel*.**

tiger   camel

5. _____   9. _____

6. _____   10. _____

7. _____   11. _____

8. _____   12. _____

Theme 2: **Nature Walk**   **185**

At the Beach

Read the paragraphs.

Brad and his family took a walk on the beach. Brad saw tiny fish in the tide pools. Then he spotted two crabs hiding near some shells. Later, he saw seagulls flying in the sky.

Brad saw people at the beach, too. Some were swimming in the water. Children were making sand castles. They used buckets and shovels.

Complete the chart with examples from the story and some of your own. Then make up your own category about the beach. Write examples for it.

Category	Examples
Animals	
Activities	

Name _____

Which Word?

Read the sentence. Read the words in the box. Circle the word that belongs in the sentence. Write it on the line.

1. The _____ swims in the lake.

| **duck   quack** |

2. Dave sat on a big _____.

| **sick   rock** |

3. Pam will _____ a cake.

| **back   bake** |

4. I made a house with _____.

| **blocks   trucks** |

5. Ed put on a _____.

| **jacket   ticket** |

6. Mom is _____ the books.

| **licking packing** |

Write two sentences. Use a circled word in each sentence.

7. _____

8. _____

Solve the Clue

Read each clue. Read the two words in each box. Circle the word that answers the clue and write it on the line.

Tiger
VCV

1. A short amount of time

_____

moment   summer

2. To keep safe

_____

follow   protect

3. A number less than ten

_____

seven   funny

4. The opposite of shut

_____

finish   open

5. Something to ride in

_____

wagon   basket

6. A small child

_____

student   baby

Write two of the circled words that have a long vowel sound in the first syllable.

_____   _____

Name _____

Which Word Fits?

Word Bank

little	idea	hear	enough	water
laugh	more	learn	people	hungry

Read each clue. Choose a word from the box that fits the clue. Write it in the puzzle.

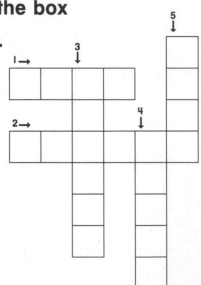

Across

1. a plan in your mind
2. men, women, and children

Down

3. as much as you need
4. opposite of teach
5. opposite of less

Write a word from the box that belongs with each group of words.

6. see, smell, _____

7. thirsty, tired, _____

8. yell, talk, _____

9. small, tiny, _____

10. milk, tea, _____

Name _____

Using Words

Read the story. Use words from the box to fill in the blanks.

The Lion and the Mouse

A _____

A lion was asleep when a little mouse ran across his paw and up to his nose. The lion woke from his nap and roared.

"Please, Lion, don't hurt me, and someday I will help you," said the mouse.

Months later, the lion found himself caught in a trap. Mouse heard his roar and ran to help.

"Now I can return your kindness," said the mouse.

With his sharp teeth, the mouse bit through the ropes and set the lion free!

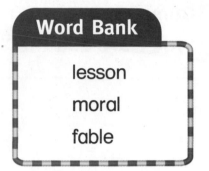

Word Bank

lesson
moral
fable

Little favors may lead to great rewards is the

_____ of this fable.

This is a good _____ to learn.

Name _____

Fable Chart

Complete the chart to tell about the fable
"The Hare and the Tortoise."

Title _____   _____
Main Characters _____   _____
What the Characters Are Like _____   _____   _____
The Moral _____   _____
The Lesson I Learned _____   _____   _____

Name _____

Comparing Fables

Use the chart below to compare the five fables.

	Characters	Main Event	Moral, or Lesson
The Hare and The Tortoise			
The Crow and the Pitcher			
The Grasshopper and the Ants			
Belling the Cat			
The Fly on the Wagon			

Tell which fable was your favorite and why you liked it.

My favorite fable is _____

I like it because _____

_____

Name _____

Writing a Fable

Plan your fable. Fill in the Fable Chart with words and phrases.

Title of Fable _____

Fable Characters

Name of Animal	How It Acts Like a Person
1. _____ _____	_____ _____
2. _____ _____	_____ _____

What Happens?

First, _____

_____

Next, _____

_____

Last, _____

_____

Moral _____

Name _____

Words Ending with **k** or **ck**

► The words **neck**, **lake**, and **ask** end with
the same sound. This sound may be
spelled **k** or **ck**.

► The vowel sound before **ck** in **neck** is short.

► The vowel sound before **k** in **lake** is long.
A silent **e** is added after **k**.

► The **k** at the end of **ask** is part of a
consonant cluster.

**Sort Write each Spelling Word under the correct
spelling for the last sound.**

Spelling Words

1. neck
2. lake
3. sick
4. ask
5. lick
6. pack
7. woke
8. kick
9. lock
10. poke

du**ck**

/k/ spelled **ck**

bi**ke**

/k/ spelled **k**

1. _____   7. _____

2. _____   8. _____

3. _____   9. _____

4. _____   10. _____

5. _____

6. _____

Name _____

Stringy Sentences

► A stringy sentence is more than one sentence joined together by **and**.

► Break a stringy sentence into shorter sentences.

► Each shorter sentence should have a naming part and an action part.

Draw a line under each stringy sentence.

1. The children read fables at school.

2. The children read fables and they write fables and they draw pictures of fables.

3. Kayla and Kim decide to write a fable about a cat and a dog.

4. The children make animal masks and they act out the fable and the masks are made from paper plates.

5. John reads a fable and draws a picture of it.

Write one of the stringy sentences above as two shorter sentences. Use capital letters and end marks.

6. _____

_____

Name _____

Fable Chart

Complete the chart to tell about another fable.

Title _____ _____
Main Characters _____ _____
What the Characters Are Like _____ _____ _____ _____
The Moral _____ _____
The Lesson I Learned _____ _____ _____

Name _____

Spelling Spree

Letter Swap Change each letter in dark print to *k*
or *ck* to make a Spelling Word. Write the word.

1. si**p**

   _____

2. **p**ole

   _____

3. lo**t**

   _____

4. la**ne**

   _____

5. ne**t**

   _____

6. ki**d**

   _____

Rhyming Clues Write a Spelling Word for
each clue.

7. It rhymes with **tack**
   It begins like **pig**. _____

8. It rhymes with **mask**
   It begins like **apple**. _____

9. It rhymes with **broke**
   It begins like **wish**. _____

10. It rhymes with **stick**
    It begins like **lamp**. _____

Spelling Words

1. neck
2. lake
3. sick
4. ask
5. lick
6. pack
7. woke
8. kick
9. lock
10. poke

Name _____

A Fable Character

An animal in a fable learns this lesson: *You do not make friends by being greedy.* How do you think the animal acts at the beginning of the fable? What does it think and say? Write some sentences about the animal that learns this lesson.

_____

_____

_____

_____

_____

Now draw a picture of the animal.

Name _____

Complete Sentences

**Turn each group of words into a sentence by adding a
naming part or an action part. Write the new sentence
to begin with a capital letter and have an end mark.**

1. a big black crow _____

_____

2. rode on the back of a wagon _____

_____

3. the speedy hare _____

_____

4. did not share the food _____

_____

5. two grasshoppers _____

_____

6. wanted to tie a bell around the cat's neck

_____

_____

Name _____

Exact Words

Cross out each underlined word, and replace it with a
more exact word from the box. Write the new word
next to it.

> **Word Bank**
>
> sleeps   bumped   screamed   hopped   splash

1. The wagon <u>went</u> _____ along the

   dusty road.

2. The turtles <u>go</u> _____ into the water.

3. The cat <u>is</u> _____ on the bed.

4. The hare <u>moved</u> _____ through the

   tall grass.

5. The boy <u>said</u>, _____ "Help me!"

**Write three sentences. Use one word from the box in
each sentence.**

6. _____

7. _____

8. _____

Syllables and Vowel Sounds

► If a vowel ends a syllable, it usually has a long sound.

► If a single vowel comes between two consonants, it usually has a short sound.

Draw a line between a syllable in Column A and a syllable in Column B to make a word. Write and read each new word.

Column A   **Column B**

1. pen   lent   1. _____

2. si   kin   2. _____

3. la   en   3. _____

4. sev   cil   4. _____

5. nap   ter   5. _____

6–10. Divide these words into syllables. Read the words.

summer

object

finish

traffic

protect

Proofreading and Writing

Proofreading Read the sentences from a fable. Circle four Spelling Words that are not spelled correctly. Write each word correctly.

Who was brave enough to put the bell around the cat's nek? It would be a hard job! The mouse would have to be very careful! She couldn't kic the cat by mistake or poke him as he slept. What would happen if the cat wok up? No one wanted to aks the old mouse to do it.

Spelling Words

1. neck
2. lake
3. sick
4. ask
5. lick
6. pack
7. woke
8. kick
9. lock
10. poke

1. _____   3. _____

2. _____   4. _____

Write a Fable Beginning On another sheet of paper, write the beginning of a fable. Use four of the spelling words. Read it to a partner. Have the partner find and check the spelling words you used.

Name _____

Unstring the Sentences

Read each stringy sentence. Write it as two shorter sentences. Use capital letters and end marks correctly.

1. My family went to the zoo and we saw a lion cub and the cub followed its mother.

   _____

   _____

2. I like to read stories and my favorite stories are about kittens and I think they are cute.

   _____

   _____

3. Ben has a cat and a bird and they are his pets and he takes good care of them.

   _____

   _____

4. Jan went to the circus and the bears did tricks and two tigers jumped through a hoop.

   _____

   _____

Name _____

Adding End Marks

Read this conversation. The sentences have no end marks. Write the end mark and the kind of sentence it is. Find two telling sentences, one command, one question, and one exclamation.

Hare: Watch me run __ _____

Tortoise: Do you want to have a race __ _____

Hare: I will race you to the pond __ _____

Tortoise: I am slow, but I can still win __ _____

Tortoise: Hooray, I won __ _____

Write your own sentences. Begin and end each sentence correctly.

1. Question: _____

_____

2. Exclamation: _____

_____

3. Command: _____

_____

Name _____

My Community

**Describe your neighborhood or community. What does
it look like? What do people like to do there? What do
you like best about your neighborhood or community?**

_____

_____

_____

_____

_____

_____

_____

**Describe a place in your neighborhood or community
that is important to you.**

_____

_____

_____

_____

Name _____

Around Town: Neighborhood and Community

Fill in the chart as you read the stories.

	What neighborhood or community places appear in this theme?	Who are some of the community helpers in this theme?
Chinatown		
A Trip to the Firehouse		
Big Bushy Mustache		
Jamaica Louise James		

Name _____

Which Word?

Circle the word that names or describes each picture.

Then use the circled word in a sentence.

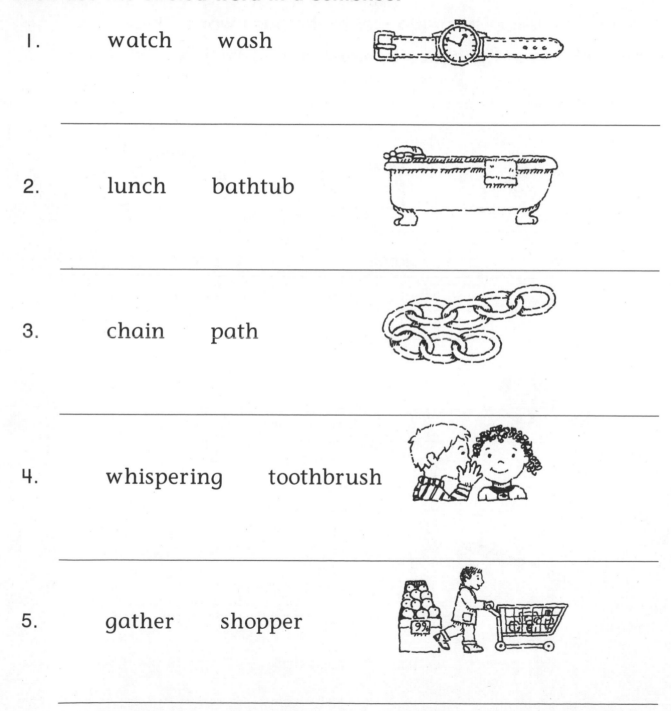

1.   watch   wash

_____

2.   lunch   bathtub

_____

3.   chain   path

_____

4.   whispering   toothbrush

_____

5.   gather   shopper

_____

Name _____

Big, Bigger, or Biggest?

**The word under the picture is a base word. On the line
under the middle box, add -er to the base word. On the
line under the last box, add -est to the base word. Then
draw pictures in the boxes to show the differences in size.**

Example:

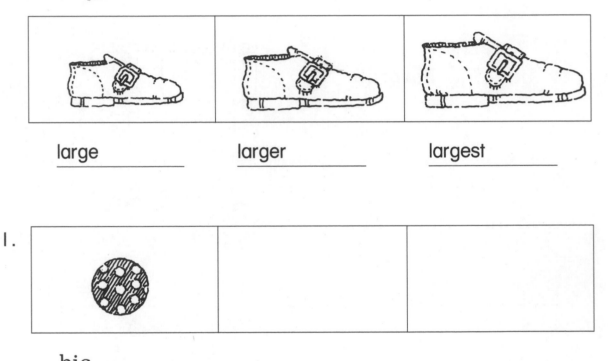

large _____   larger _____   largest _____

1.

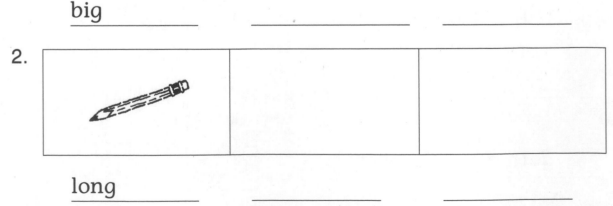

big _____   _____   _____

2.

long _____   _____   _____

Name _____

Matching and Sorting Words

Draw a line from each word to its meaning.

1. during	the season after fall
2. heard	throughout a certain time
3. lion	a large wild cat
4. winter	took in sounds with the ears

Word Bank

during	heard	lion	winter

Think how the words in each group are alike. Then choose one word from the box to add to each group of words below.

5. seen, smelled, _____

6. before, after, _____

7. summer, spring, _____

8. tiger, panther, _____

Use two of the words from the box in sentences.

9. _____

10. _____

Name _____

Words to Draw

Draw a picture of someone making a delivery at an apartment. Then use each vocabulary word, *delivery* and *apartment*, in a sentence.

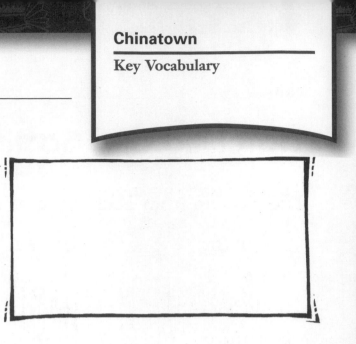

1. _____

2. _____

Draw a picture of people using handcarts at a market. Then use each vocabulary word, *handcarts* and *market*, in a sentence.

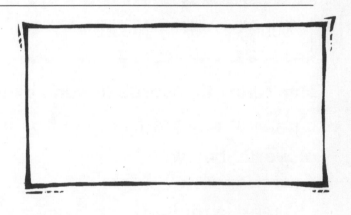

3. _____

4. _____

Draw a picture of a celebration. Then use the vocabulary word *celebration* in a sentence.

5. _____

Name _____

What I Like Chart

As you read the story, choose pages that show things you like to see in Chinatown. Write the page number and a sentence next to it.

What I Like to See in Chinatown

page _____	
page _____	
page _____	
page _____	
page _____	
page _____	
page _____	
page _____	

Name _____

Two Letters—One Sound

Each Spelling Word is spelled with **th**, **wh**, **sh**, or **ch**. Each pair of letters stand for one sound.

► the **th** sound ⟶ **th**at, mo**th**er, smoo**th**
► the **wh** sound ⟶ **wh**y, some**wh**at
► the **sh** sound ⟶ **sh**e, friend**sh**ip, wi**sh**
► the **ch** sound ⟶ **ch**ild, sear**ch**ing, ri**ch**

1. when
2. sheep
3. both
4. then
5. chase
6. teeth
7. teach
8. dish
9. which
10. than
11. wash
12. catch*

Write each Spelling Word under the word with the same sound. The sound may be at the beginning, middle, or end of the word.

whale   **chair**

_____   _____

thumb

_____   _____

_____

ship

_____   _____

_____

_____

Who? What? Where?

All of the words in the box are naming words, or nouns. Nouns name people, places, and things.

Complete the chart below. Write words from the box to show which nouns name people, places, and things.

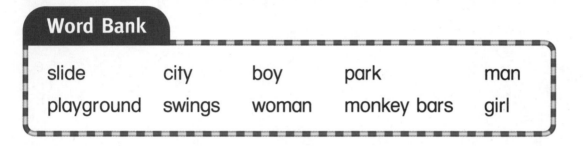

Word Bank

slide	city	boy	park	man
playground	swings	woman	monkey bars	girl

People	Places	Things
1. _____	5. _____	8. _____
2. _____	6. _____	9. _____
3. _____	7. _____	10. _____
4. _____		

Name _____

Organizing a Story Scene

Write your ideas for a story scene.

Setting — Where does the scene take place?

_____

_____

Characters — Which characters are in the scene?

_____

_____

Actions or Events — What happens in the scene?

_____

_____

Retelling the Story

Finish each sentence about Chinatown.

1. The person telling this story is _____

_____

2. Tai chi is _____

_____

3. The grandmother makes special soup when

it gets cold outside because _____

_____

4. The boy can barely move in the outdoor

market because _____

_____

5. The boy in the story will march in the parade

next year because _____

_____

Name _____

Making Judgments

Read the story below.

Cowhands

Hank and Charlie are cowhands on a small cattle ranch. Their job is to herd the cows to town to be sold. This means that they must keep the cattle moving in the right direction. They do this by riding their horses beside the herd.

It is a long, dusty ride on the trails to town. Sometimes the dust is very thick. Hank and Charlie wear scarves called bandannas over their noses and mouths to keep the dust out. No matter how dusty it gets, Hank and Charlie must keep track of every cow.

When the sun goes down, Hank and Charlie find a place to camp. The cattle rest for the night. Hank and Charlie cook their dinner over a campfire. A delicious smell fills the air. The two cowhands are tired after a day of hard work. They spread out their sleeping bags and lie down under the stars. The camp is quiet. After a while Hank and Charlie hear a coyote howling in the distance. They both fall asleep as the coyote sings its song.

Making Judgments continued

After you have read the story "Cowhands," complete the chart below.

I Would / Would Not Like Chart

Things the Characters Do	I Would/Would Not Like This	Reasons Why I Feel This Way
1. _____ _____	_____ _____	_____ _____
2. _____ _____	_____ _____	_____ _____
3. _____ _____	_____ _____	_____ _____
4. _____ _____	_____ _____	_____ _____
5. _____ _____	_____ _____	_____ _____

Name _____

Spelling Spree

Word Fun **Think how the words in each group are alike. Write the missing Spelling Words.**

1. goats, horses, _____

2. rinse, scrub, _____

3. glass, fork, _____

4. lips, tongue, _____

5. throw, bounce, _____

6. learn, school, _____

1. when
2. sheep
3. both
4. then
5. chase
6. teeth
7. teach
8. dish
9. which
10. than
11. wash
12. catch*

Write the two Spelling Words that rhyme with each other.

7. _____

8. _____

Name _____

Knowing Your ABC's

Read the words in each box. Write the five words in ABC order.

Word Bank

| most | morning | move | mother | month |

1. _____   4. _____

2. _____   5. _____

3. _____

Word Bank

| restaurant | read | remember | report | rent |

6. _____   9. _____

7. _____   10. _____

8. _____

Theme 3: **Neighborhood and Community**   221

Double the Fun

Use the double consonants in the box to finish each word.
Then write the word on the line.

ck	ff	ll	ss

duck   cuff   ball   dress

1. sme____ _____

2. po____et _____

3. gra____ _____

4. waterfa____ _____

5. sna____ _____

6. ski____ _____

7. gla____ _____

8. sni____ing _____

9. cla____ _____

10. cli____ _____

Proofreading and Writing

Proofreading **Read the sentences below. Find
and circle four Spelling Words that have spelling
mistakes. Write them correctly.**

1. Buth Grandma and I love to go to Chinatown.

2. We have a hard time deciding wich seafood restaurant we like best.

3. It is fun to watch the fish in the fish tank chace each other.

4. There is no fish fresher thun the fish in Chinatown.

Spelling Words

1. when
2. sheep
3. both
4. then
5. chase
6. teeth
7. teach
8. dish
9. which
10. than
11. wash
12. catch*

_____   _____

_____   _____

**Writing Sentences On a separate sheet of paper, write
four sentences that tell about a place you like to visit.
Use Spelling Words from the list.**

Name _____

Spotlight on Naming Words

Naming words are called nouns. Nouns name
people, places, and things.

**Read each sentence. Underline the nouns that name
people. Circle the nouns that name things. Draw a box
around the nouns that name places.**

1. The baby is in the swing.

2. The pencil and paper
   belong to the student.

3. The family is at the beach.

4. The books are on the
   shelves in the library.

Name _____

To Be Exact

**Write each sentence. Replace the underlined
word with a more exact noun.**

Example:

I visited my aunt at her **place**.
I visited my aunt at her **house**.

1. My aunt and I went to an outdoor <u>place</u> to buy

   food. _____

2. There were many different kinds of fresh <u>foods</u>

   there, such as apples and oranges. _____

   _____

3. My aunt bought three pounds of <u>fruit</u> to make a

   pie. _____

4. She paid the <u>person</u> for the fruit we bought.

   _____

5. When we got to my aunt's house, she made the pie

   and baked it in the <u>thing</u>. _____

   _____

Name _____

Revising a News Story

Read the newspaper story. When possible, combine two sentences into one to make the story sound better.

Chinese New Year

Chinatown — Today was the Chinese New Year. People who live in Chinatown celebrated. Visitors celebrated. Adults crowded the streets. Children crowded the streets. Boys from the kung fu school marched down the streets. Girls from the kung fu school marched down the streets. The dragon parade was exciting to watch. The lion dance was exciting to watch. The dragon costumes were beautiful. The lion costume was beautiful. Everyone had a good time.

_____

_____

_____

_____

_____

Name _____

Revising Your Friendly Letter

**Decide how to make your writing better. Put a check next
to the sentences that tell about your letter.**

Superstar

☐ I used all five parts of a friendly letter.
(date, greeting, body, closing, my name)

☐ My topic is interesting to the reader.

☐ I used details and exact words.

☐ My letter clearly tells how I feel.

☐ I used different kinds of sentences, and
there are few mistakes.

Rising Star

☐ My letter does not have all five parts.

☐ My topic may not interest the reader.

☐ I need more details and exact words.

☐ My letter does not show how I feel.

☐ My sentences are too much the same and
have many mistakes.

Name _____

Different Kinds of Sentences

Read each sentence. Then write each sentence with the correct end mark.

1. I am very happy

   _____

2. Did you find my puppy

   _____

3. We went for a walk

   _____

4. This is a big surprise

   _____

Write a telling sentence about a dog.

_____

_____

Name _____

Spelling Words

These Spelling Words are words that you use in your writing. Look carefully at how they are spelled. Write the missing letters in the Spelling Words below. Use the words in the box.

1. n___m___   7. wh___t

2. o___   8. t_____

3. t_____e   9. d___

4. w_____t   10. l___tt_____

5. m___s_____f   11. t___

6. w___nt   12. b_____n

Spelling Words

1. of
2. do
3. to
4. what
5. write
6. myself
7. name
8. time
9. went
10. been
11. too
12. little

Write the Spelling Words below.

_____   _____

_____   _____

_____   _____

_____   _____

_____   _____

_____   _____

Name _____

Spelling Spree

Choose a Spelling Word to complete each sentence. Write the words in the puzzles.

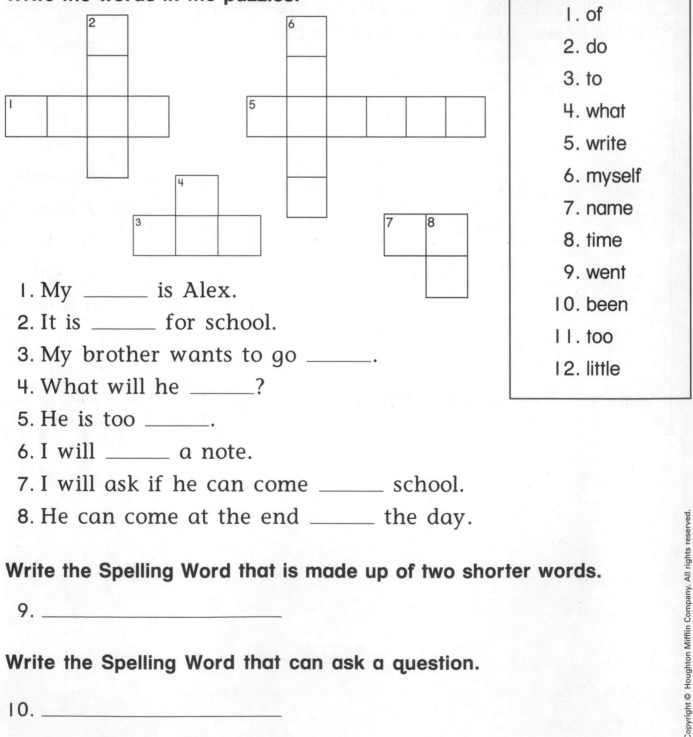

1. of
2. do
3. to
4. what
5. write
6. myself
7. name
8. time
9. went
10. been
11. too
12. little

1. My _____ is Alex.
2. It is _____ for school.
3. My brother wants to go _____.
4. What will he _____?
5. He is too _____.
6. I will _____ a note.
7. I will ask if he can come _____ school.
8. He can come at the end _____ the day.

Write the Spelling Word that is made up of two shorter words.

9. _____

Write the Spelling Word that can ask a question.

10. _____

Name _____

Proofreading and Writing

Proofreading Find and circle misspelled Spelling Words below. Then write each word correctly.

Dear Akimi,

    It has not ben a good day. I whent to a new school. I did not know anyone in my class. I did not know whut to answer when the teacher asked me a question. I ate lunch by miself. In the afternoon I had to rite a story about my day.

Your friend,
Benita

1. _____   4. _____

2. _____   5. _____

3. _____

Write and Draw a Community Poster On construction paper, write the name of a community helper. Then write sentences that tell how that person helps. Use as many Spelling Words as you can.

Name _____

Train Play

Write the word that goes with each sentence.

Word Bank

| train | waited | spray | stay | day | paid |

1. Our class went to visit a fire station one _____.

2. We had to ride a _____ to get there.

3. The teacher _____ for our tickets.

4. We _____ for the train for ten minutes.

5. We had to _____ together when we walked.

6. We helped the firefighters _____ water on the trucks to wash them.

Now write each word under the train that has the same vowel pair.

pail   may

_____   _____

_____   _____

_____   _____

Name _____

Compound Word Find

Underline the compound words. Then write three sentences to finish the letter. Use words in the box to make compound words. Use those words in your letter.

Word Bank

| day | flash | body | light | some | every |

Dear Grandmother,

Our new neighbor is a firefighter. Her

name is Ms. Sanchez.

She let me visit the fire station yesterday.

I took my notebook so I could take lots of notes.

Ms. Sanchez showed me the water truck, the

ambulance, and the ladder truck. They were

parked in the firehouse driveway.

_____

_____

_____

Name _____

Word Clues

Write a word from the box to complete the sentences.

Word Bank

clothes   guess   order

Find out what job Cal wants to do when he grows up. Read the clues to find out. Write the answer on the last line.

1. He wants to help people.

2. He will wear _____ that keep him safe from a fire. He will wear a big helmet, rubber boots, and a heavy coat.

3. He will drive a big truck.

4. He will help keep the buttons, knobs, and water hoses on his truck in working _____.

    Can you _____ what job Cal wants to do? _____

Name _____

Firefighter Words

Write a word or words from the box to tell what each sentence describes.

Vocabulary

chief	gear	emergencies
firefighters	dispatch	fire engine

1. I am a truck with a siren and lights.

   _____

2. I tell the people what to do. _____

3. Air tanks and an ax can be very

   helpful. _____

4. We race to the fire and put it out.

   _____

5. Fires are burning and people need help.

   _____

6. When a message arrives, help is soon on

   the way. _____

Name _____

Firehouse Chart

Complete the chart below as you read the story.

Topic

A Trip to the Firehouse

F I R E   D E P A R T M E N T

Main Idea

The firefighters show the

children many exciting things.

Detail _____

Detail _____

Detail _____

Detail _____

Detail _____

Name _____

ai or *ay?*

Most of the words have the long **a** sound spelled **ay** or **ai**.

    the long **a** sound ——→ **way, train**

▶ The word **they** is special. The vowels **ey** spell the long **a** sound in **they**.

▶ The word **great** is special. The vowels **ea** spell the long **a** sound in **great**.

Write each Spelling Word under the hat with the matching letters.

<table>
<tr><td colspan="2">**Spelling Words**</td></tr>
<tr><td>1.</td><td>train</td></tr>
<tr><td>2.</td><td>way</td></tr>
<tr><td>3.</td><td>mail</td></tr>
<tr><td>4.</td><td>play</td></tr>
<tr><td>5.</td><td>trail</td></tr>
<tr><td>6.</td><td>pay</td></tr>
<tr><td>7.</td><td>sail</td></tr>
<tr><td>8.</td><td>hay</td></tr>
<tr><td>9.</td><td>nail</td></tr>
<tr><td>10.</td><td>rain</td></tr>
<tr><td>11.</td><td>they*</td></tr>
<tr><td>12.</td><td>great*</td></tr>
</table>

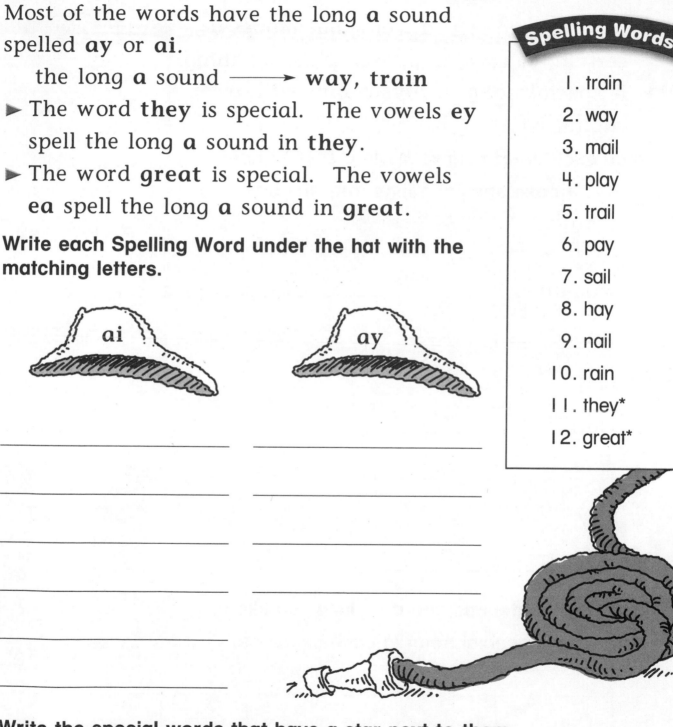

ai

ay

_____
_____
_____
_____

Write the special words that have a star next to them.

_____

Name _____

Names of Nouns

▶ A special noun is a word that names a certain, or special, person, place, or thing.

▶ A special noun always begins with a capital letter.

Read each noun below. Write a special noun for it. Choose special nouns from the box.

1. park _____

2. woman _____

3. bridge _____

4. dog _____

5. state _____

6. river _____

7. city _____

8. man _____

Write two sentences about a place you like to visit. Use a special noun in each sentence.

_____

_____

_____

Web Notes

Read the paragraph. Write your notes about the paragraph in the web.

Fire Safety Rules

Suppose you are in a building that catches fire. First stay calm. Warn everyone in the building about the fire. Be careful though, you must get out quickly. Feel doors to see if they are hot. If they are, the fire may be burning on the other side. See if there is another way out. Once you are out, call the firefighters. Never go back inside a burning building.

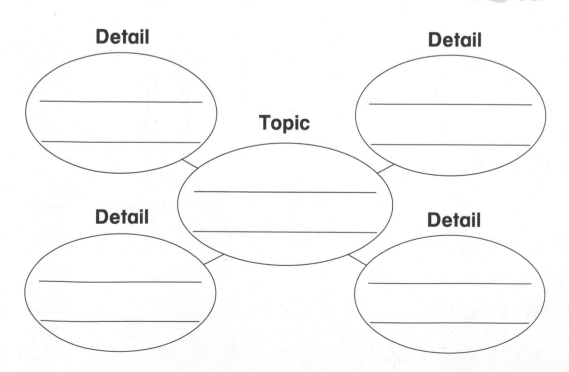

Detail

Detail

Topic

Detail

Detail

Theme 3: **Neighborhood and Community**   239

Name _____

A Firefighter Is Talking

Pretend you are a firefighter. You are being asked questions on a TV show.

Write your answers on the lines.

1. What kind of gear do firefighters wear?

1. _____

_____

_____

2. Why is there a pole in a firehouse?

2. _____

_____

_____

3. What happens in the dispatch room in a firehouse?

3. _____

_____

_____

4. Why is it important to make sure all the equipment works?

4. _____

_____

_____

What's the Idea?

Read the newspaper story.

House Catches Fire

There was a fire in the kitchen of the Reese family home Thursday morning. The house is at 4301 Oak Line Drive. Two neighbors saw thick smoke coming through a window. One neighbor ran to her house to call 911. She told the emergency operator where the fire was. Another neighbor ran to the Reese house. She helped everyone in the family get out of the house safely.

The emergency operator called the fire station. A water truck and a fire engine were dispatched. The firefighters got to the Reese house within ten minutes. The firefighters hooked long hoses up to the water truck. They aimed the water at the fire. Soon, the fire was out. Everyone was safe because of the neighbors and the work of the firefighters.

The Reese family was happy that no one was hurt. The Reese family thanked the firefighters. They also thanked their neighbors.

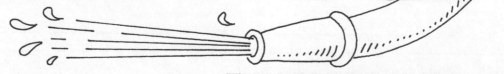

Name _____

What's the Idea? continued

Use the newspaper story about the fire at the Reese home to complete the chart below.

Topic: _____

Main Idea: _____

_____

Detail 1: _____

_____

Detail 2: _____

_____

Detail 3: _____

_____

Detail 4: _____

_____

Spelling Spree

Maze Play Connect the words with the long *a* sound to help the fire truck get to the fire.

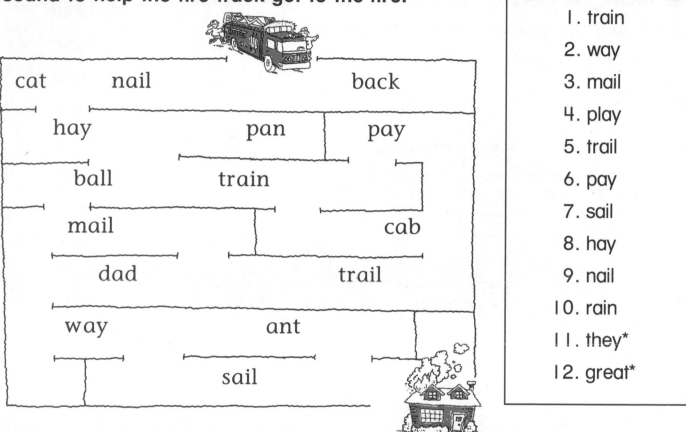

cat   nail   back

hay   pan   pay

ball   train

mail   cab

dad   trail

way   ant

sail

Spelling Words

1. train
2. way
3. mail
4. play
5. trail
6. pay
7. sail
8. hay
9. nail
10. rain
11. they*
12. great*

Write each Spelling Word in the maze under its long *a* spelling.

ai   ay

1. _____   6. _____

2. _____   7. _____

3. _____   8. _____

4. _____

5. _____

Name _____

Dictionary Word Match

Read the word list. Write each word under the
place where you would find it in the dictionary.
Would the word be found in the beginning,
middle, or end?

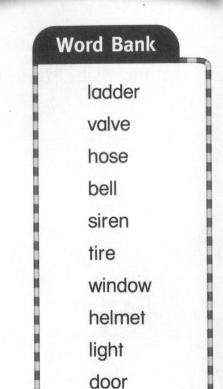

Word Bank

ladder

valve

hose

bell

siren

tire

window

helmet

light

door

Beginning

A–K

Middle

L–S

End

T–Z

_____ _____ _____

_____ _____ _____

_____ _____ _____

_____

Consonant Choice

Write the word that completes each sentence.

1. Clang! Clang! The fire engine

   _____ down the street.

showed   rushed

2. The firefighters wanted to

   _____ the fire in a hurry.

reach   chain

3. The fire engine stopped at a plant

   _____.

ship   shop

4. There was a fire burning in a

   _____.

wheelbarrow   whale

5. Many people stopped to _____
   the firefighters work.

watch   check

6. _____ quickly pulled out
   the water hoses.

Those   They

7. The firefighters sprayed water

   _____.

when   everywhere

8. The store owner _____ the
   firefighters before they left.

thought   thanked

Name _____

Proofreading and Writing

Proofreading Circle the four Spelling Words that are wrong in this letter. Then write each word correctly.

Spelling Words

1. train
2. way
3. mail
4. play
5. trail
6. pay
7. sail
8. hay
9. nail
10. rain
11. they*
12. great*

Dear Chief Rogers,

  We had a grate time at the fire station! It was fun to pla with Spot, the firehouse dog. Everyone liked washing the fire truck too. The way the water came out of the hose looked like ran. I liked watching the firefighters get ready to go fight a fire. Thay dressed really fast. May I come visit another day?

    Sincerely,
    Tony

_____   _____

_____   _____

Write What You Want to See
What would you like to see if you could visit a firehouse? Write it on a separate sheet of paper. Use Spelling Words from the list.

Name Those Facts

► A special noun is a word that names a certain, or special, person, place, or thing.

► A special noun always begins with a capital letter.

special person

special place

special thing

Complete each sentence with a special noun that tells about you.

1. My name is _____.

2. My street address is _____.

3. The name of my teacher is _____.

4. My favorite place to eat is _____.

5. My favorite story is called _____.

Name _____

Making It Clear

Read the dialogue. Then rewrite the Caller's answers.
Add special nouns that give exact information.

Emergency Operator: 911 Operator.
Caller: There is a fire at a store.

_____

_____

Emergency Operator: What is the address?
Caller: The store is near a busy street.

_____

_____

Emergency Operator: What is your name?
Caller: Pam.

_____

_____

Emergency Operator: Where are you now?
Caller: I'm looking out the window of a house.

_____

_____

Emergency Operator: Stay where you are. Help
will be there in a few minutes.

Name _____

Special Names

Replace the words in dark print with special names.
Write the names on the lines below.

Dear Joan,

Today was a very exciting **day**. **My friend**
and I were walking down **the street**. A fire
truck came racing past us. It stopped at the
house of **our neighbor**. We ran to see what was
wrong. We found that **a cat** was stuck in a tree.

Yours truly,

Meg

1. _____

2. _____

3. _____

4. _____

5. _____

On the lines, write a sentence about a friend of
yours. Use a special name in your sentence.

6. _____

_____

Name _____

Letter Magic

Change one letter in each word in dark print to
make a new word that will finish each sentence.
Each new word should have the letters
ow or *ou* in it.

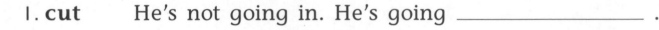

1. **cut**   He's not going in. He's going _____ .

2. **cot**   That's not a pig. That's a _____ .

3. **load**   She's not being quiet. She's being _____ .

4. **horse** That's not a barn. That's a _____ .

5. **flowed** That's not a tree. That's a _____ .

6. **short** Speak softly. Don't _____

**Look at the words you wrote. Choose one word that
has the letters *ou* and one word that has the letters *ow*.
Write a sentence with each of those words.**

7. _____

8. _____

Name _____

Suffix Fun

Write the base word of each underlined word.

1. Sarah likes her <u>colorful</u> costume. _____

2. She feels <u>playful</u> when she puts it on. _____

3. On the stage, she has to sing <u>loudly</u>. _____

4. But at home she sings <u>quietly</u> to herself. _____

5. She had to learn her songs <u>quickly</u>. _____

6. She is <u>thankful</u> she has a good part in the play.

_____

Add *-ly* or *-ful* to the words below to make new words.

7. silent _____

8. skill _____

9. hope _____

10. sad _____

Name _____

Use the Words

Word Bank

behind	soldier	story

Answer each riddle with a word from the box.

1. I have a beginning and an end. What am I? _____

2. I keep our country safe. Who am I? _____

3. I mean the opposite of "in front." _____

Write a short story about a soldier who sees a horse behind a tree. Use all of the words from the box in your story.

_____

_____

_____

_____

_____

Name _____

Costume Play

José is in the school play. Follow these directions to show how José will look.

Directions:

1. Draw the costume of a king on José. Include a crown.
2. Draw a bushy beard.
3. Draw a big mustache.

José and his mom are talking. Use the words in the box to complete their sentences.

> ### Vocabulary
>
> handsome   disguise   mirror

Mom: "What a _____ king we have here!"

José: "I'm not really a king. I'm wearing a _____."

Mom: "Then who are you?"

José: "I'm José, your son."

Mom: "You'd better look in a _____ to be sure!"

Name _____

Problem-Solving Event Map

As you read the story, complete the Problem-Solving Event Map below.

Problem: Ricky loses the _____ his teacher gave him.

What Ricky Tries	Predict: Will this solve the problem?	Check: Does this work?
_____ _____	Yes No	_____
_____ _____	Yes No	_____
_____ _____	Yes No	_____
_____ _____	Yes No	_____
_____ _____	Yes No	_____

Name _____

The Vowel Sound in cow

The words **town** and **house** have the same vowel sound. This vowel sound may be spelled **ow** or **ou**. The words **could** and **should** do not follow this rule.

Spelling Words

1. town
2. house
3. sour
4. frown
5. cow
6. clown
7. found
8. how
9. mouse
10. brown
11. could*
12. should*

Write the Spelling Words with the *ow* sound spelled *ow*.

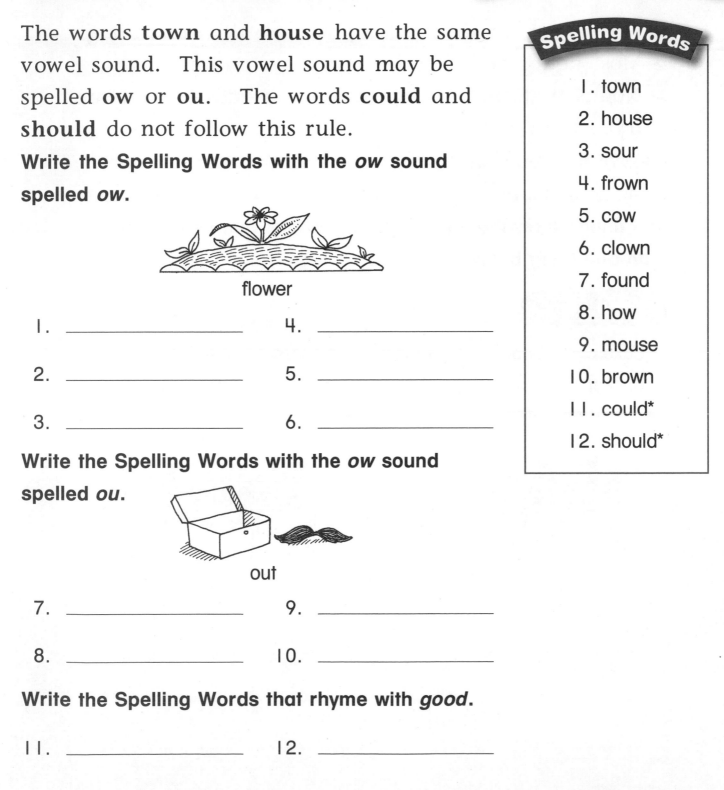

flower

1. _____   4. _____

2. _____   5. _____

3. _____   6. _____

Write the Spelling Words with the *ow* sound spelled *ou*.

out

7. _____   9. _____

8. _____   10. _____

Write the Spelling Words that rhyme with *good*.

11. _____   12. _____

Name _____

Which Is Which?

▶ Nouns can name one thing or more than one thing.

▶ Most nouns add -**s** to name more than one.

▶ Nouns that end in **s**, **x**, **ch**, and **sh** add -**es** to name more than one.

Look at the nouns in the box. Some name one thing and some name more than one thing. Write the nouns that name one thing below the flag. Write the nouns that name more than one thing below the group of flags.

Word Bank

| boxes | shoes | dishes | dresses | mustache |
| pocket | apples | wish | fox | father |

_____   _____

_____   _____

_____   _____

_____   _____

_____   _____

What Is the Problem?

Think of a problem that you have had. How did
you solve it? What did you learn from the problem
and the solution? Use this chart to help you
organize your ideas about the problem.

1. What was the problem? How did it come up?

_____

_____

2. How did you solve the problem?

_____

_____

3. What did you learn from solving the problem?

_____

_____

Name _____

True or Not True?

Print the word *True* or *Not true* after each sentence.

1. Ricky was happy that he looked like his mother. _____

2. Mrs. Cortez asked the children to leave their costumes in their desks. _____

3. Ricky looked older with his mustache on. _____

4. Ricky told his father all about the lost mustache. _____

5. Ricky tried to make his own mustache. _____

6. Ricky's father shaved his mustache so he would look more like Ricky. _____

7. Ricky's new mustache was a special gift from his father. _____

Find each sentence that was *Not true*. On the lines below, rewrite each sentence to make it true.

8. _____

9. _____

   _____

10. _____

    _____

Problem-Solving

Read the story. Then complete the chart on the next page.

The Cookie Problem

Mike's class wanted to do something special for the children at the hospital. They decided to raise money to buy books. They would have a cookie sale at school. Everyone would bring cookies to sell.

When he got home, Mike asked his mother for help making cookies. She reminded him that she had to go to work soon.

Mike asked his father for help. His father wanted to help, but he had promised to help Mike's sister build her science project.

Mike decided to count his money. He had been saving to buy a new model to build. He could buy cookies, but then he would have to wait even longer to get the model.

Then Mike had an idea. He called his friend Tran. They could make cookies together! Tran's grandfather would help them. Mike took sugar and flour to Tran's house. Mike and Tran and Tran's grandfather made cookies. The next day, the class sold cookies. They used the money to buy ten books for the children at the hospital.

Name _____

Problem-Solving continued

After you've read the story "The Cookie Problem," answer this question.

What is Mike's problem?

_____

In the box on the left, write each solution Mike tries. In the box on the right, write why it doesn't work.

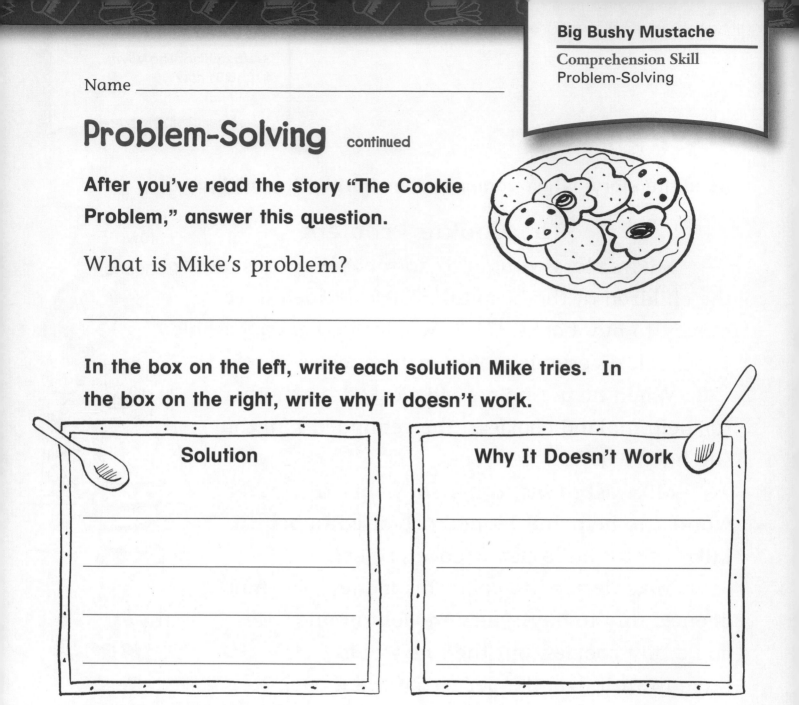

Solution	Why It Doesn't Work

Mike's last solution does work. Write the solution and why it works.

_____

_____

Do you think Mike's solution is a good one? Why or why not?

Spelling Spree

Spelling Scramble Unscramble the letters to make a Spelling Word.

1. town
2. house
3. sour
4. frown
5. cow
6. clown
7. found
8. how
9. mouse
10. brown
11. could*
12. should*

1. **w n o r f** ___ ___ ___ ___ ___

2. **s d u o h l** ___ ___ ___ ___ ___ ___

3. **u s o h e** ___ ___ ___ ___ ___

4. **w o r n b** ___ ___ ___ ___ ___

5. **u o l d c** ___ ___ ___ ___ ___

6. **w n l c o** ___ ___ ___ ___ ___

Fill-in Fun Write the missing Spelling Word to create a pair of words that go together.

7. sweet and _____

8. lost and _____

9. _____ and country

10. cat and _____

Name _____

Search for Meaning

Read each sentence. Use the context to figure out what the underlined word means. Write the letter for the meaning of the word on the line next to each sentence.

____ 1. When our team scored the winning point, the fans cheered for our victory.

____ 2. We celebrated by inviting all of our friends to eat cake and sing.

____ 3. We rushed home so we could be the first ones there for the party.

____ 4. Rosie lost her hat, so she retraced her steps and looked everywhere she had been.

____ 5. My mother's special creation for the party was a drink she made from ice cream, pineapple, and bananas.

Meanings

A. went back over

B. win or getting first place

C. something made up

D. had a party for a special reason

E. went quickly

Play Day

Choose the word with *ai* or *ay* that correctly completes each sentence. Write the word on the line.

1. Ray has a part in the school _____ . | play   jail |

2. He can't _____ to act on the stage. | stay   wait |

3. Ray has one of the _____ parts. | main   hay |

4. He has to _____ his lines many times to remember them. | main   say |

5. After the show is over, everyone will _____ Ray's hard work. | gray   praise |

6. _____ he will even be the star of the play! | faintly   maybe |

Write two sentences of your own. Use an *ai* word in one sentence and an *ay* word in the other.

_____

_____

Name _____

Proofreading and Writing

Proofreading Circle four Spelling Words that are
spelled wrong in this note. Then write each word
correctly.

Dear Parents,

For the school play, could you help us
with costumes? Here's what we need:

► A tail for the couw

► Big shoes for the cloun

► Broun pants and shirt for the mowse

Thank you for your help!

Mr. Jackson

Spelling Words

1. town
2. house
3. sour
4. frown
5. cow
6. clown
7. found
8. how
9. mouse
10. brown
11. could*
12. should*

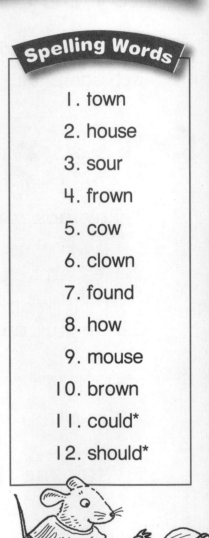

1. _____   3. _____

2. _____   4. _____

Write a Letter Pretend you have just been in a play
about Cinco de Mayo. On a separate piece of paper,
write a letter to a friend. Tell about the play. Use
Spelling Words from the list.

What Do You See?

Remember:
- ► Nouns can name one thing or more than one thing.
- ► Most nouns add **-s** to name more than one.
- ► Nouns that end in **s**, **x**, **ch**, and **sh** add **-es** to name more than one.

Write what you see in each spot. The first one has been done for you.

apple

mustache

dress

I see <u>two apples</u>   I see _____   I see _____

_____.   _____.   _____.

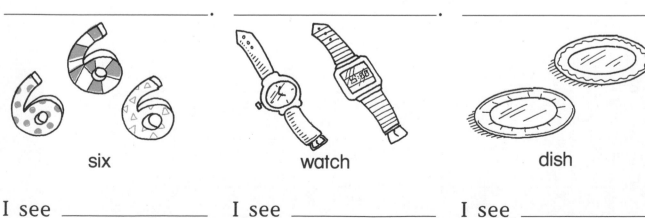

six

watch

dish

I see _____   I see _____   I see _____

_____.   _____.   _____.

Name _____

Solving a Problem

Read the school newspaper report. It tells about a play put on by the second grade. Make the writing more interesting by replacing the underlined words with exact nouns. Write your choices for exact nouns on the lines below.

Last night, the second grade put on a play. The <u>teacher</u> said it was about Cinco de Mayo. <u>Two children</u> played <u>instruments</u>. <u>One girl</u> told the story. All the students wore costumes. Boys wore sombreros and carried <u>things</u>. Girls wore skirts and serapes. When the play ended, everyone clapped.

1. _____

2. _____

3. _____

4. _____

5. _____

Name _____

Where's That Mustache?

Remember:

► Nouns can name one thing or more than one thing.

► Most nouns add **-s** to name more than one.

► Nouns that end in **s**, **x**, **ch**, and **sh** add **-es** to name more than one.

Suppose Ricky wrote a report about his lost mustache. He made five mistakes in his report. Circle his mistakes. Then write each word correctly.

I lost my mustache. I looked everywhere for it. I looked in my pocketes. I looked in the boxs in my closet. I looked under the dishs. I looked under the chaires in the kitchen. I even looked under the benchs in the park. Then my mother surprised me with a new mustache!

1. _____   4. _____

2. _____   5. _____

3. _____

Name _____

Rhyme Time

Here are some poems about painting. Finish each poem.
Write a word from the box that rhymes with the last word in
the first sentence.

Word Bank

dream	easy	sea	street	week

1. The beach is a place where I like to be.

   That's where I go when I paint the _____.

2. Things are not always what they seem.

   Today I'll paint a funny _____.

3. Here's a painting of a dog with furry feet.

   He's walking down a busy _____.

4. How can I paint on a day that's breezy?

   That's a job that won't be _____!

5. At this painting you may not peek.

   You will have to wait a _____.

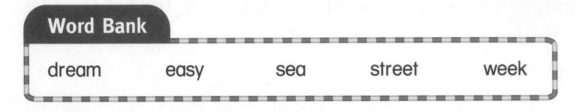

Name _____

What Do You See?

Choose a word from the box to label each picture.

Word Bank

celebration   furniture   lotion   nature   picture   vacation

_____   _____

_____   _____

_____   _____

Name _____

I Believe in Art

The Lady with
the Flowers

Grammy Spends
the Whole Evening Sewing

I Can't Believe I Ate the
Whole Thing!

Write the name of the painting to answer each question.

1. Which painting shows someone with a needle and thread?

   _____

2. Which painting shows someone sitting in front of an empty plate?

   _____

3. Which painting shows someone carrying roses?

   _____

Make your own drawing called _I Believe in Happiness_.

I Believe in Happiness

Name _____

Subway Words

Maria is new to the city. She asks her friend Lulu how to get around. Finish the sentences with words from the box.

Vocabulary

booth   plaque   station   subway   token

Maria: How can I get around in the city?

Lulu: You can use the _____.

Maria: Where can I go to find it?

Lulu: You will find a _____ close to your house.

Maria: Then what do I do?

Lulu: You go down the stairs and find a _____ where you buy a _____. Then you get on the train.

Maria: How do I know where to get off?

Lulu: When the train slows down, look out the window. You will see a _____ with the name of the station on it.

Jamaica Louise James

Graphic Organizer Making
Inferences Chart

I Can Use Clues Chart

As you read, use clues from the story to make guesses
about what Jamaica and the other people in the story
are like. Write your guesses and the clues on the chart.

Story: Jamaica Louise James

What the Character Is Like	Story Clues
_____	_____
_____	_____
_____	_____
_____	_____
_____	_____
_____	_____
_____	_____
_____	_____

Name _____

E? Ea? Ee?

The vowel sound in **we**, **keep**, and **clean** is
the long **e** sound. The long **e** sound may be
spelled **e**, **ee**, or **ea**.

► The words **people** and **the** do not follow
this pattern.

**Write the Spelling Words with the long *e* sound
spelled *e*.**

_____ _____

**Write the Spelling Words with the long *e* sound
spelled *ee*.**

_____ _____ _____

**Write the Spelling Words with the long *e* sound
spelled *ea*.**

_____ _____ _____

_____ _____

Write the two Spelling Words you have not written.

_____ _____

Spelling Words

1. clean
2. keep
3. please
4. feel
5. we
6. be
7. eat
8. tree
9. mean
10. read
11. the*
12. people*

Name _____

Which Word?

Choose the best word for each sentence and write it on the line.

1. Jamaica often plays with

   other _____.

   | child   children |

2. One _____ gave her a
   flower.

   | child   children |

3. Jamaica painted the _____
   with the green hat.

   | woman   women |

4. The four _____ in the subway
   liked her paintings.

   | man   men |

5. One _____ said the paintings
   made her feel happy.

   | woman   women |

6. A _____ who was an artist
   looked at the paintings.

   | man   men |

7. One _____ gave Jamaica
   a big hug.

   | woman   women |

8. The _____ at Jamaica's school
   went to see her paintings.

   | child   children |

Get Ready to Write Your Ad

Use this form to help you write your ad. Remember that you are trying to convince someone to buy your product. Think about who might buy it and what you could say to convince them to buy it.

James Advertising Agency

Name of what I'm going to sell: _____

Who will buy it? _____

Tell about the person who will buy it. _____

_____

_____

Tell why your product is special. _____

_____

Name two reasons why someone should buy it.

_____

_____

How Does It Feel?

Read each sentence. Choose the word that best completes the sentence. Write the word on the line.

Word Bank

| worried | mad | excited | proud | happy | scared |

1. Grammy and Mama are _____ about their birthday present for Jamaica. They want her to open it quickly.

2. Jamaica is _____ about how much the present cost.

3. Grammy is not _____ to work at night, but Jamaica is afraid of the night.

4. The grown-ups in the subway always look so _____.

5. Grammy is very _____ when she sees Jamaica's paintings.

6. Now the people in the subway seem _____. They like Jamaica's presents.

Making Inferences

Read the story. Then answer the questions on page 278.

Luann's House

Luann lives with her Aunt Sonya and Uncle Leo on the top floor of their building. Luann's best friend lives next door. Her name is Carla.

Luann has three pets. She has a gerbil in a small cage, a parrot in a big cage, and a cat that likes to go on the roof. Luann gives her gerbil balls of cotton to make into nests. She feeds the parrot pieces of fruit and slices of bread. When Luann and Carla go up to the roof, Luann brings her cat.

Uncle Leo reads in a big chair with a light behind it. Sometimes he reads to Carla and Luann about the new paintings at the museum.

Aunt Sonya has a garden on the roof. She grows roses. She knows the names of all the roses. Sometimes she brings fresh bread and iced tea up to the roof for the girls.

Name _____

Making Inferences continued

Use the things you know about Luann from the story to answer the questions. Do the same with Uncle Leo and Aunt Sonya.

1. What is special about Luann?

   _____

   _____

   _____

Luann

2. What kind of person is Uncle Leo?

   _____

   _____

   _____

Uncle Leo

3. Would you like Aunt Sonya to take
   care of you for an afternoon? Why?

   _____

   _____

   _____

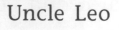

Aunt Sonya

Spelling Spree

Rhyming Clues Write a Spelling Word
for each clue.

1. It begins with the letter **e**.

   It rhymes with **seat**. _____

2. It begins with the letters **tr**.

   It rhymes with **see**. _____

3. It begins with the letter **w**.

   It rhymes with **he**. _____

4. It begins with the letter **r**.

   It rhymes with **bead.** _____

5. It begins with the letter **b**.

   It rhymes with **me**. _____

6. It begins with the letters **cl**.

   It rhymes with **bean.** _____

7. It begins with the letter **k**.

   It rhymes with **deep**. _____

8. It begins with the letter **m**.

   It rhymes with **lean.** _____

Spelling Words

1. clean
2. keep
3. please
4. feel
5. we
6. be
7. eat
8. tree
9. mean
10. read
11. the*
12. people*

Theme 3: **Neighborhood and Community**   **279**

Name _____

Where to Find It

Word Bank

lap	laugh	drove	dream
drip	lamb	late	drum
law	dry	dress	land

**Look at the dictionary guide words below. Write each
word from the box on the correct dictionary page.**

draw / drive

_____

_____

_____

drop / duck

_____

_____

_____

lake / large

_____

_____

_____

last / lazy

_____

_____

_____

Riddle Fun

Find two words from the box that go together to match each description.

Word Bank

clown	cow	growling	frowning
house	mouse	loud	prowling

1. A place where there is lots of noise

   _____

2. A small animal sneaking around

   _____

3. A funny guy at the circus who is unhappy

   _____

4. An angry animal that gives milk

   _____

Proofreading and Writing

Proofreading Circle four Spelling Words that are spelled wrong. Then write each word correctly.

1. clean
2. keep
3. please
4. feel
5. we
6. be
7. eat
8. tree
9. mean
10. read
11. the*
12. people*

New Artist in Town

Many peaple came to see th paintings of Jamaica Louise James yesterday. She paints the things around her. She paints her family, houses, cats, and dogs. One special painting is a picture of a tree. Her paintings make us all feal happy. Pleese don't miss her wonderful show of paintings! The show will be open for one more day.

1. _____   3. _____

2. _____   4. _____

Write a Review On a separate sheet of paper, write about a painting you have seen. Tell what you like about the painting. Use Spelling Words from the list.

One or More Than One

Write the word that goes with each drawing.

Word Bank

men	mice	woman	mouse
teeth	man	tooth	women

1. _____

2. _____

3. _____

4. _____

5. _____

6. _____

7. _____

8. _____

Theme 3: **Neighborhood and Community**   283

Name _____

Who Will Use It?

Here are three items for sale. On each line, write who might buy the item. Then read what the ad might say. Circle the best phrase for each ad.

Who will use it?

_____

Easy to Use!

Dries in 2 Days

Child-proof Bottle

Who will use it?

_____

Smells Like Bubble Gum!

Makes Shaving Easy!

Great for Art Projects!

Who will use it?

_____

Fresh Smell of Hay!

Smell Like a Rose Garden!

Attracts Bees Like Daisies Do!

Name _____

What's the Plural?

**Circle the five words that are not correct. Then write
each word correctly.**

March 3, 2001

    Today I saw three womans wearing big
hats. The hats had bright yellow flowers on
them. I saw two childs playing in the park.
They had pet mouses that crawled up their
arms. I wonder if a mouse has sharp tooths.
Then I saw four mans carrying a piano. Their
faces were red.

1. _____

2. _____

3. _____

4. _____

5. _____

Shopping Words

Write each word from the box next to its correct definition.

Vocabulary

| deliveries | grand opening | success |
| flyer | grocery store | supermarket |

1. a printed ad that is given to many people

1. _____

2. ending with a good outcome

2. _____

3. packages that are brought to the home

3. _____

4. a party to mark the opening of a new store

4. _____

5. stores for buying food, milk, and other household goods

5. _____

_____

On a separate sheet of paper, draw a flyer for the grand opening of a grocery store. Tell the time, the date, and the name of the store.

Name _____

Compare Community Stories

Fill in the chart as you read the stories.

	Grandpa's Corner Store	Barrio: José's Neighborhood
Where does the selection take place?	_____ _____ _____ _____	_____ _____ _____ _____
Who are the main characters?	_____ _____	_____ _____
What are the important events or details?	_____ _____ _____ _____ _____	_____ _____ _____ _____ _____

Name _____

What Do You Think?

**Answer the questions about the characters and places
in the theme. Tell what you think and why.**

1. Would Lucy like Jamaica's idea for Grammy's birthday
   present? Why or why not?

   _____

   _____

2. Lucy's gift to Grandpa and Jamaica's gift to
   Grammy made the community better. What
   might make your community better? Why?

   _____

   _____

3. Chinatown and Lucy's neighborhood are special places.
   What things make your community special?

   _____

   _____

4. Ricky wore the mustache home and lost it. If you were
   in a play, would you wear your costume home? Explain.

   _____

   _____

Name _____

Celebration Words

**Use words from the box to complete the sentences.
Write each word in the puzzle.**

Vocabulary

fiesta   customs   harvest   barrio   traditions

Across

3. People follow the same ____ at Thanksgiving year
   after year.

5. The ____ is a big party in the community.

Down

1. Many people from
   the ____ speak
   Spanish.

2. We study the ____
   of people around
   the world.

4. In the fall, they
   ____ the crops from
   the garden.

Name _____

Compare Them

Read each sentence. Choose the word that correctly completes it.

1. The blue jay is _____ than the robin.

| louder | loudest |

2. My dad's raincoat is the

_____ one in our family.

| bigger | biggest |

3. The gray crayon is _____ than the yellow one.

| shorter | shortest |

4. The _____ moves along the path slower than the turtle.

| chain | snail |

5. Which of these _____ is smaller?

| trays | plays |

6. The sailboat with the green sail is the _____ in the race.

| faster | fastest |

7. They _____ that this must be the hottest day of the year.

| complain | delay |

8. The _____ train of all those in the station has six cars.

| longer | longest |

Name Those Nouns

Read each sentence. Circle the naming words.

1. My friends live nearby.

2. They live in a big city.

3. What is their street called?

4. Sometimes they walk to school.

5. Their teacher is really nice.

**Write each naming word you circled. Then
write a special noun for each naming word.**

1. _____   _____

2. _____   _____

3. _____   _____

4. _____   _____

5. _____   _____

Name _____

Spelling Review

Write Spelling Words to answer the questions.

1–8. Which words are spelled with **th**, **wh**, **sh**, or **ch**?

1. _____   5. _____

2. _____   6. _____

3. _____   7. _____

4. _____   8. _____

9–17. Which words that you haven't written have the long **a** or long **e** sound?

9. _____   14. _____

10. _____   15. _____

11. _____   16. _____

12. _____   17. _____

13. _____

18–20. Which words have the vowel sound in **cow**?

18. _____   19. _____   20. _____

Spelling Words

1. tray
2. when
3. teeth
4. than
5. be
6. eat
7. sheep
8. play
9. frown
10. sail
11. chase
12. teach
13. please
14. train
15. wash
16. which
17. found
18. we
19. tree
20. mouse

Name _____

Solve This

Read the passage. Then answer the questions.

"Tomorrow is Wear Something Silly Day at school," Marcy told her mom. "I want to wear something silly, but I don't know what to wear."

Marcy looked in her closet. Then she looked in the attic. She couldn't find anything that was silly enough.

"I have an idea," she told her mom. Marcy turned her clothes inside out. Then she put them on backwards.

"That's really silly!" Mom said. "What a great idea!"

1. What is Marcy's problem?

_____

2. What does she try first?

_____

3. Why doesn't it work?

_____

4. How does she solve the problem?

_____

Name _____

Find It Fast

**Read the words. Write each word under the place
where you would find it in a dictionary. Is it at the
beginning, the middle, or the end?**

Word Bank

zoo	pet	fruit	apartment	theater
tree	swing	school	hospital	

Beginning	**Middle**	**End**
A–K	**L–S**	**T–Z**

_____   _____   _____

_____   _____   _____

_____   _____   _____

**Now list the words that are found at the end of
a dictionary in ABC order.**

_____

_____

_____

Name _____

Spelling Spree

Hidden Words Circle the Spelling Word hidden in each group of letters below. Write the word on the line.

1. frown
2. teach
3. tree
4. sheep
5. which
6. mouse
7. we
8. play
9. sail
10. found

1. lpmouseto _____

2. qtreemba _____

3. arlfrownp _____

4. vgiwhich _____

5. fsheepmse _____

Rhyming Clues Write a Spelling Word for each clue.

6. It rhymes with **round**.
   It begins like **fan**. _____

7. It rhymes with **beach**.
   It begins like **table**. _____

8. It rhymes with **gray**.
   It begins like **plate**. _____

9. It rhymes with **be**.
   It begins like **worm**. _____

10. It rhymes with **mail**.
    It begins like **sun**. _____

Name _____

How Many?

Write what you see in each box.

1. _____

3. _____

2. _____

4. _____

Use a word from the box to complete each sentence.

5. The _____ ate seeds
   and nuts.

mouse	mice

6. A shark has many sharp

   _____ in its mouth.

tooth	teeth

7. I helped one _____ by
   walking her puppy.

woman	women

8. Five _____ played on
   the swings.

child	children

Name _____

Around Town:
Neighborhood and
Community: Theme 3
Wrap-Up

Spelling Review

Proofreading and Writing

Proofreading Circle four Spelling Words that are wrong. Then write each word correctly.

Come to a block party! It will bea this Friday. Come enjoy good things to eet. Bring the whole family, plese!

The party starts at five P.M. It will end wen you want to go home!

1. _____ 3. _____

2. _____ 4. _____

A Party Plan Write Spelling Words to complete this plan.

Dad, take the early 5._____ home. Mom,

6._____ the vegetables for the party and put them

on a 7._____. Maya, don't let the dog

8._____ the cat! T.J., brush your 9._____.

We'll have more fun 10._____ we've ever had!

Write a Diary Entry Write a diary entry about the block party. Use another sheet of paper. Use the Spelling Review Words.

Name _____

Test Practice

**Read each question about *Barrio: José's
Neighborhood.* Make a chart on a separate piece of
paper, and then write your response on the lines below.
Use the three steps you have learned. Use the checklist to make
your response better.**

1. Would you like to live in José Luís's neighborhood?
   Explain why or why not.

_____

_____

_____

_____

_____

_____

_____

Personal Response Checklist

✔ Did I repeat words from the question at the beginning of my response?

✔ Can I add more details from what I read?

✔ Can I add more of my thoughts, feelings, or experiences?

✔ Did I use clear handwriting? Did I make any mistakes?

Continue on page 300.
Theme 3: **Around Town**   299

Test Practice continued

2. **Connecting/Comparing** Think about the neighborhoods in **Barrio** and in **Chinatown.** Tell one detail that is similar to your neighborhood and one detail that is different.

_____

_____

_____

_____

_____

_____

Personal Response Checklist

✔ Did I repeat words from the question at the beginning of my response?

✔ Can I add more details from what I read?

✔ Can I add more of my thoughts, feelings, or experiences?

✔ Did I use clear handwriting? Did I make any mistakes?

Read your responses to Questions 1 and 2 aloud to a partner. Then discuss the questions on the checklist. Make any changes that will make your responses better.

Name _____

What Am I?

Write the word that answers each riddle.

Word Bank

furniture	moisture	nature
collection	vacation	imagination

1. I'm all you need when you make-believe.

   What am I? _____

2. You see me when you hike in the woods.

   What am I? _____

3. Some of us are chairs, tables, and beds.

   What are we? _____

4. I am tiny drops of water. What am I? _____

5. I am what you have in the summer when there's

   no school. What am I? _____

6. I am a group of rocks, stamps, or other things

   that are alike. What am I? _____

Name _____

Making Inferences

Read the sentences and answer the questions.

Luis looks in the box. His eyes open wide and
he starts to jump up and down. "I can't believe
it!" he exclaims. "I've always wanted a puppy."

1. How does Luis feel? What clues help you know?

_____

_____

Erin is sitting on the bus. An older woman
gets on and can't find a seat. Erin stands up and
gives the woman her seat.

2. What kind of person is Erin? What clues help you know?

_____

_____

"Wake up, Gus!" calls Dad. "It's time to get
ready for school."

"Okay," whispers Gus. He yawns, rolls over,
and falls back asleep.

3. How does Gus feel? What clues help you know?

_____

My Handbook

Contents

Trace and write the letters.

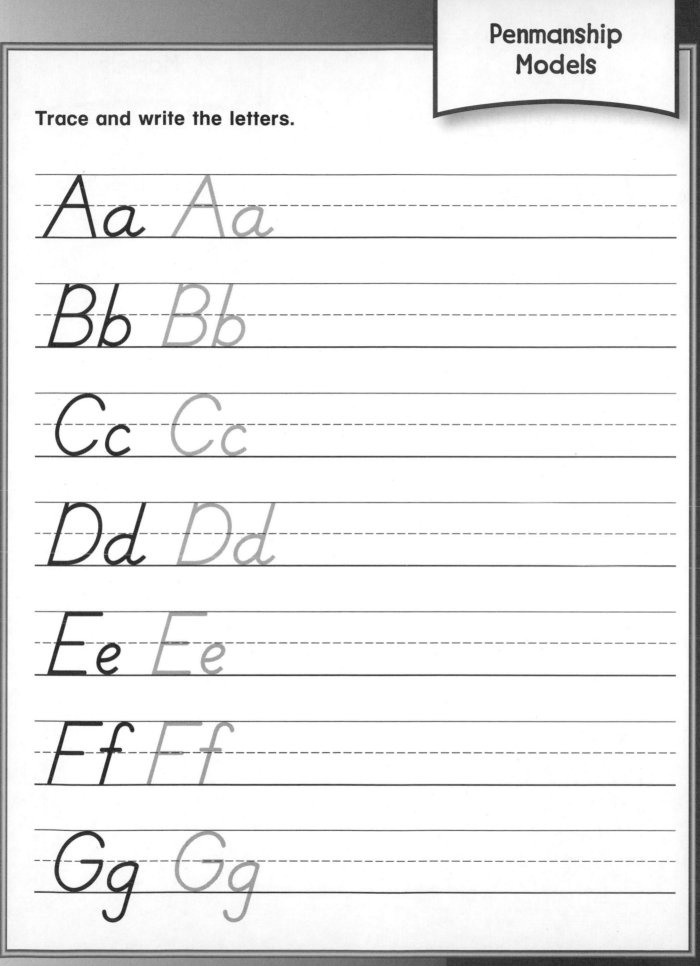

Trace and write the letters.

Hh Hh

Ii Ii

Jj Jj

Kk Kk

Ll Ll

Mm Mm

Trace and write the letters.

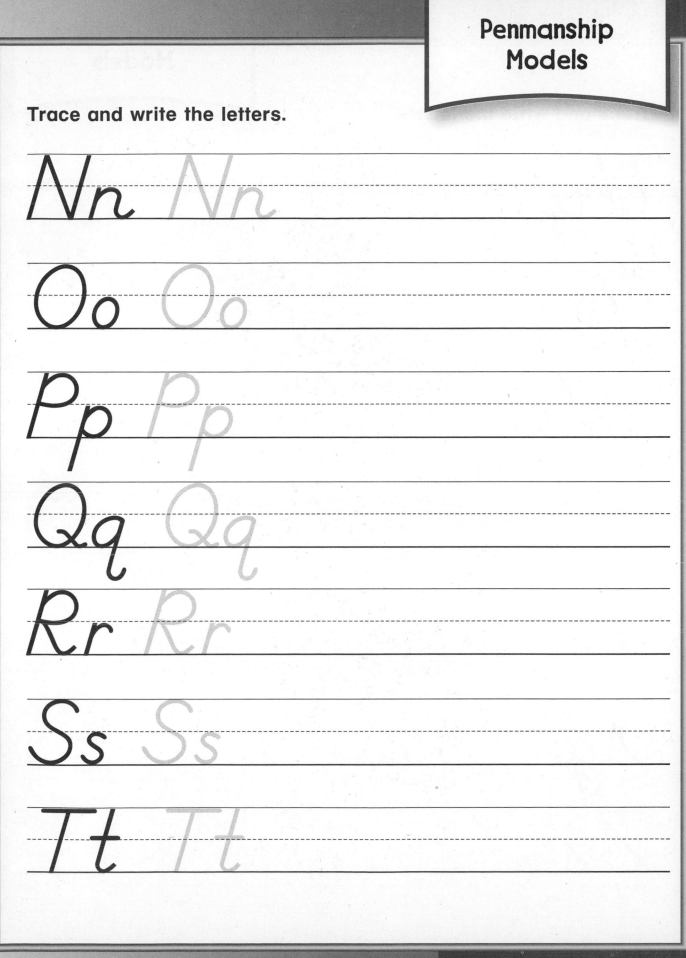

Trace and write the letters.

Uu Uu

Vv Vv

Ww Ww

Xx Xx

Yy Yy

Zz Zz

Trace and write the letters.

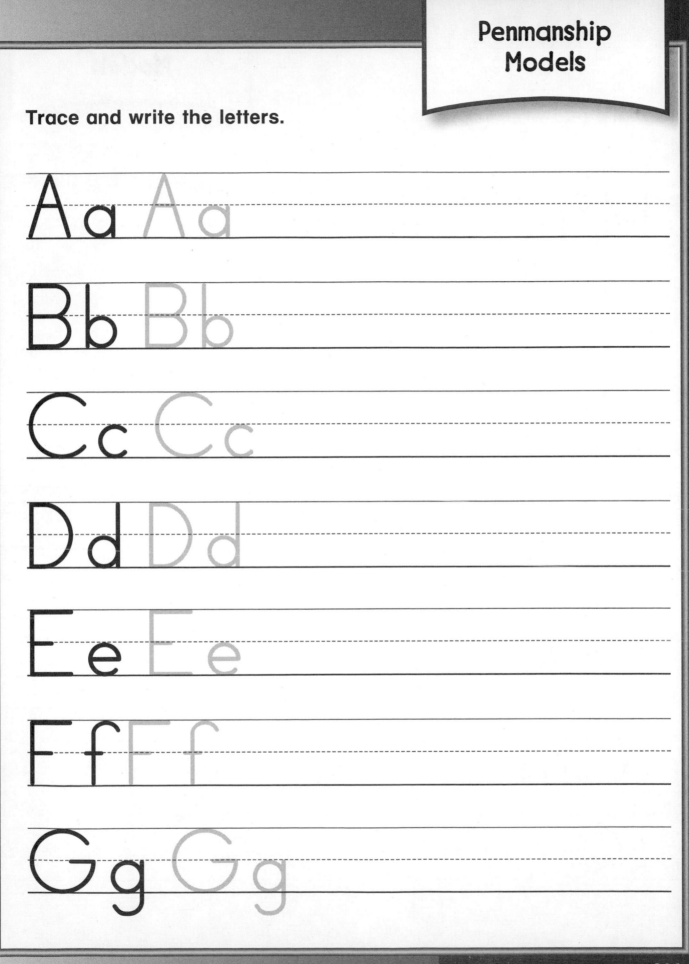

Aa Aa

Bb Bb

Cc Cc

Dd Dd

Ee Ee

Ff Ff

Gg Gg

Trace and write the letters.

Hh Hh

Ii Ii

Jj Jj

Kk Kk

Ll Ll

Mm Mm

Trace and write the letters.

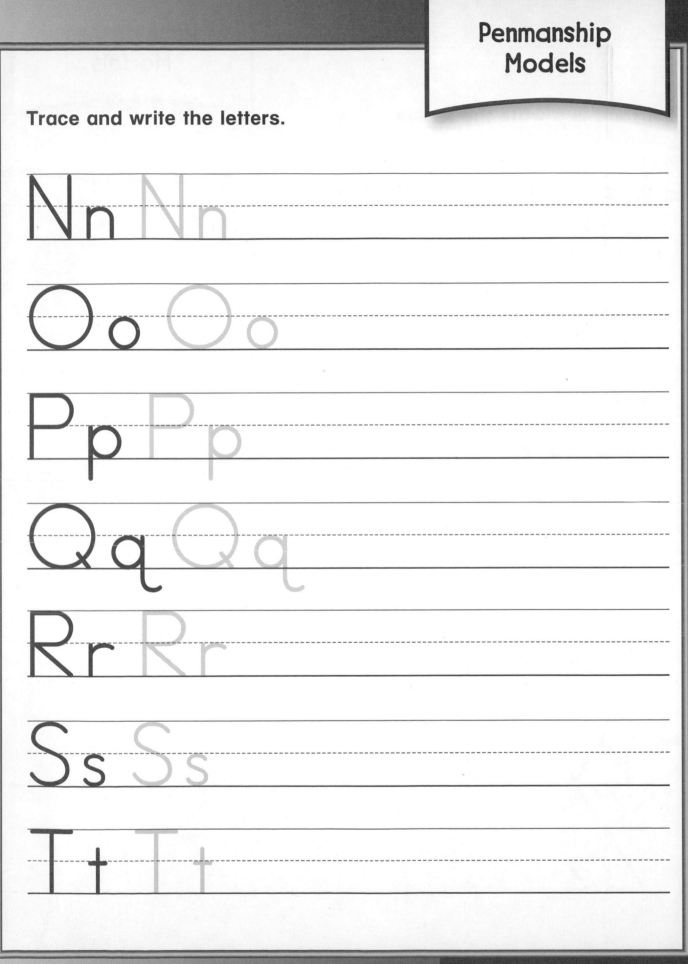

Trace and write the letters.

Uu Uu

Vv Vv

Ww Ww

Xx Xx

Yy Yy

Zz Zz

How to Study a Word

1. LOOK at the word.

► What does the word mean?

► What letters are in the word?

► Name and touch each letter.

2. SAY the word.

► Listen for the consonant sounds.

► Listen for the vowel sounds.

3. THINK about the word.

► How is each sound spelled?

► Close your eyes and picture the word.

► What other words have the same spelling patterns?

4. WRITE the word.

► Think about the sounds and the letters.

► Form the letters correctly.

5. CHECK the spelling.

► Did you spell the word the same way it is spelled in your word list?

► Write the word again if you did not spell it correctly.

A
about
again
a lot
always
am
and
any
are
around
as

B
back
because
been
before

C
cannot
caught
come
coming
could

D
do
does
done
down

E
enough

F
family
first
for
found
friend
from

G
getting
girl
goes
going

H
has
have
heard
her
here
his
how

I
I'd
if
I'll
I'm
into

it
it's

K
knew
know

L
letter
little

M
many
more
my
myself

N
name
never
new
now

O
of
off
on
once
one
other
our
outside

P
people
pretty

R
really
right

S
said
school
some
something
started
stopped

T
that's
the
their
there
they
thought
through
time
to
today
too

tried
two

V
very

W
want
was
went
were
what
when
where
who
will
would
write

Y
you
your

Silly Stories:
Reading-Writing Workshop

Look carefully at how these words are spelled.

Spelling Words

1. the	7. it
2. will	8. they
3. have	9. as
4. was	10. my
5. you	11. off
6. said	12. any

Challenge Words

1. because
2. family

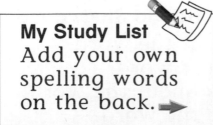

My Study List
Add your own spelling words on the back. ➡

Dragon Gets By

The Short *a* and Short *i* Sounds

short **a** sound ➡ **a**m
b**a**g

short **i** sound ➡ **i**s
d**i**g

Spelling Words

1. bag	7. ran
2. win	8. if
3. is	9. dig
4. am	10. sat
5. his	11. was
6. has	12. I

Challenge Words

1. scratch
2. picnic

My Study List
Add your own spelling words on the back. ➡

Take-Home Word List

Name_____

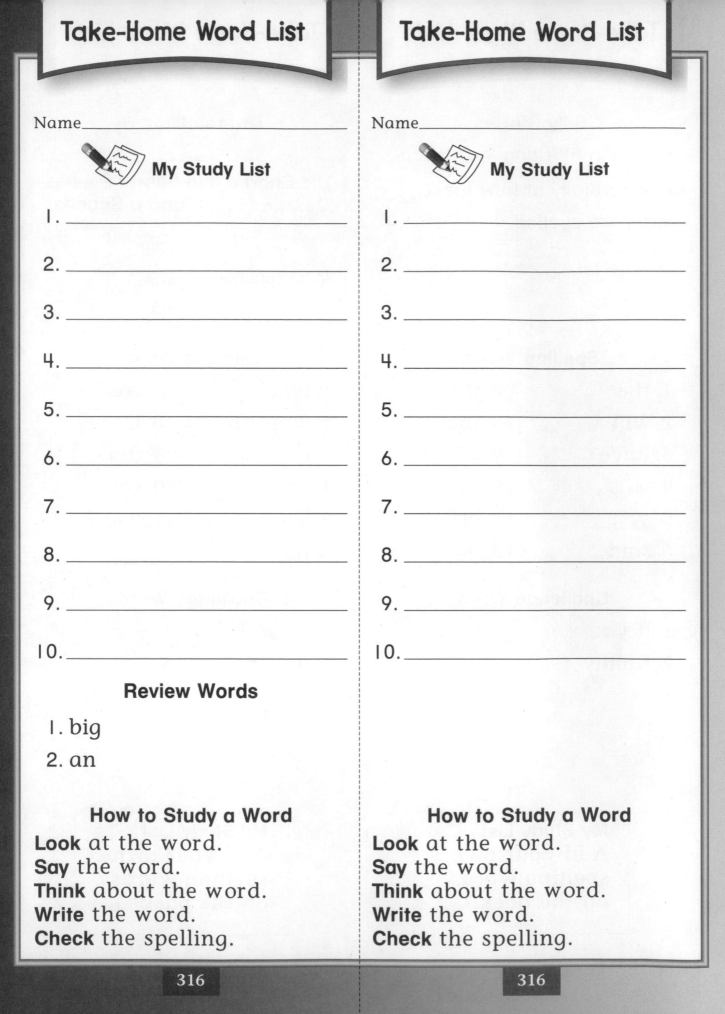

My Study List

1._____

2._____

3._____

4._____

5._____

6._____

7._____

8._____

9._____

10._____

Review Words

1. big
2. an

How to Study a Word

Look at the word.
Say the word.
Think about the word.
Write the word.
Check the spelling.

316

Take-Home Word List

Name_____

My Study List

1._____

2._____

3._____

4._____

5._____

6._____

7._____

8._____

9._____

10._____

How to Study a Word

Look at the word.
Say the word.
Think about the word.
Write the word.
Check the spelling.

316

Mrs. Brown Went to Town

Vowel-Consonant-*e* Spellings

long **a** sound ➡ **late**

long **i** sound ➡ b**ite**

Spelling Words

1. bite	7. fine
2. late	8. same
3. size	9. hide
4. made	10. line
5. side	11. give
6. ate	12. have

Challenge Words

1. shake
2. write

Julius

The Short *e, o,* and *u* Sounds

short **e** sound ➡ w**e**t, l**e**g

short **o** sound ➡ j**o**b, m**o**p

short **u** sound ➡ n**u**t, f**u**n

Spelling Words

1. fox	7. went
2. wet	8. mop
3. nut	9. hug
4. job	10. from
5. leg	11. any
6. fun	12. of

Challenge Words

1. block
2. every

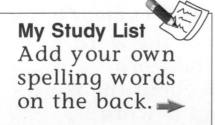

My Study List
Add your own
spelling words
on the back. ➡

My Study List
Add your own
spelling words
on the back. ➡

Take-Home Word List

Name_____

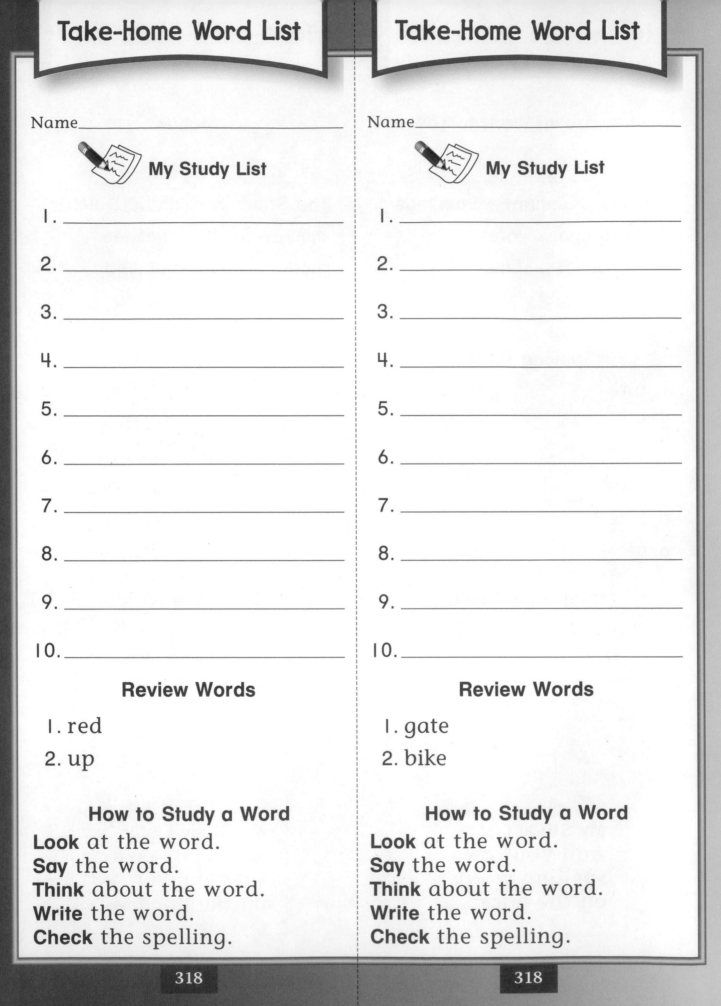

My Study List

1. _____
2. _____
3. _____
4. _____
5. _____
6. _____
7. _____
8. _____
9. _____
10. _____

Review Words

1. red
2. up

How to Study a Word

Look at the word.
Say the word.
Think about the word.
Write the word.
Check the spelling.

318

Take-Home Word List

Name_____

My Study List

1. _____
2. _____
3. _____
4. _____
5. _____
6. _____
7. _____
8. _____
9. _____
10. _____

Review Words

1. gate
2. bike

How to Study a Word

Look at the word.
Say the word.
Think about the word.
Write the word.
Check the spelling.

318

Henry and Mudge and the Starry Night

More Vowel-Consonant-*e* Spellings

long **e** ➡ th**ese**

long **o** ➡ b**one**

long **u** ➡ **use**

Spelling Words

1. bone
2. robe
3. use
4. these
5. rope
6. note
7. cute
8. close
9. hope
10. those
11. one
12. goes

Challenge Words

1. drove
2. mule

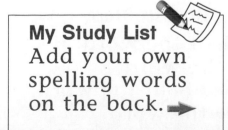

My Study List
Add your own spelling words on the back. ➡

Silly Stories
Spelling Review

Spelling Words

1. am
2. dig
3. fox
4. nut
5. leg
6. hide
7. late
8. ran
9. job
10. fun
11. wet
12. bite
13. made
14. ate
15. sat
16. mop
17. hug
18. went
19. size
20. his

Challenge Words

1. scratch
2. block
3. every
4. shake
5. write

My Study List
Add your own spelling words on the back. ➡

Name_____

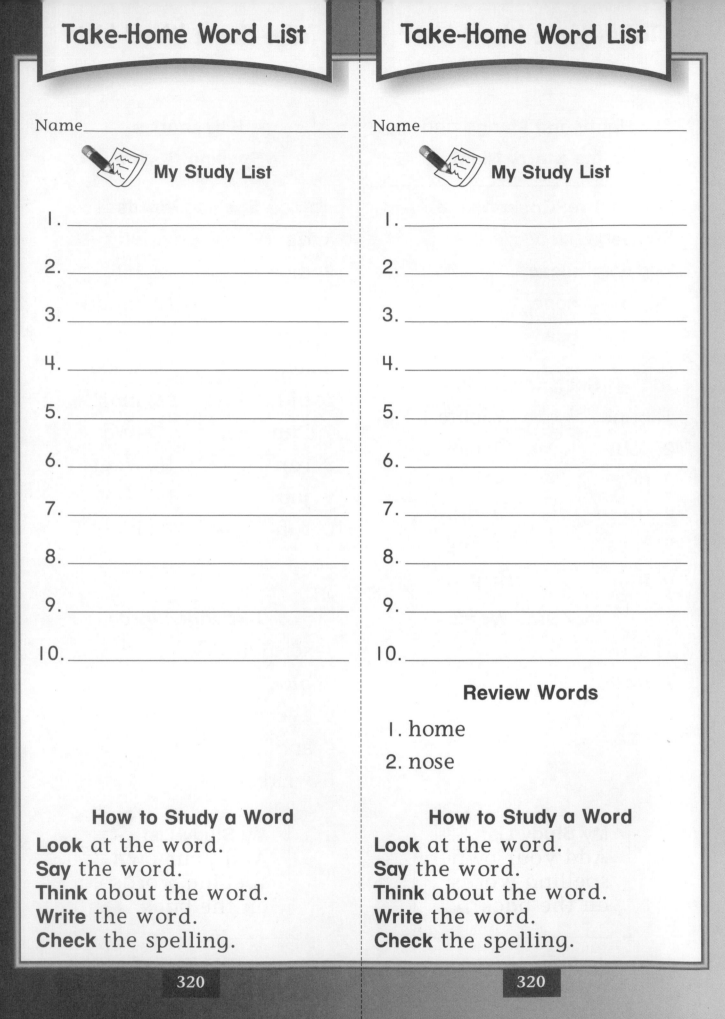

My Study List

1._____
2._____
3._____
4._____
5._____
6._____
7._____
8._____
9._____
10._____

How to Study a Word

Look at the word.
Say the word.
Think about the word.
Write the word.
Check the spelling.

320

Name_____

My Study List

1._____
2._____
3._____
4._____
5._____
6._____
7._____
8._____
9._____
10._____

Review Words

1. home
2. nose

How to Study a Word

Look at the word.
Say the word.
Think about the word.
Write the word.
Check the spelling.

320

Exploring Parks with
Ranger Dockett

Words with Consonant Clusters
trip, **sw**im, **st**ep, **cl**ub,
ne**xt**, **br**ave, **gl**ad

Spelling Words

1. trip
2. swim
3. step
4. nest
5. club
6. stone
7. next
8. brave
9. glad
10. lost

Challenge Words

1. space
2. storm

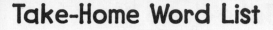

My Study List
Add your own
spelling words
on the back. ➡

Nature Walk
Reading-Writing Workshop

**Look carefully at how these
words are spelled.**

Spelling Words

1. on
2. am
3. if
4. from
5. his
6. her
7. come
8. want
9. does
10. goes
11. their
12. there

Challenge Words

1. really
2. caught

My Study List
Add your own
spelling words
on the back. ➡

Name_____

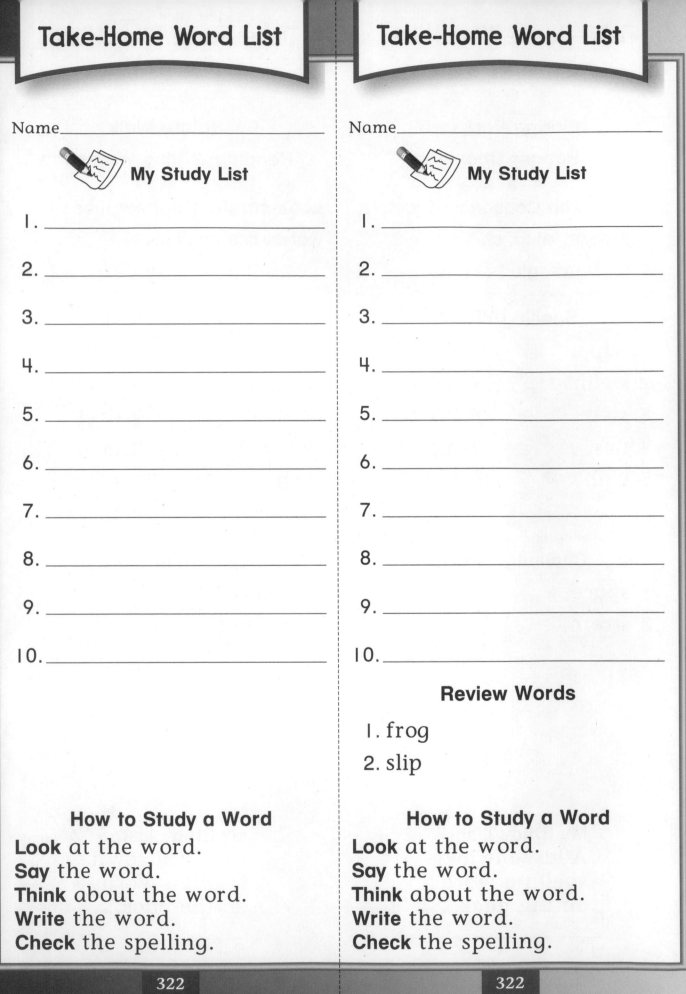

My Study List

1. _____

2. _____

3. _____

4. _____

5. _____

6. _____

7. _____

8. _____

9. _____

10. _____

How to Study a Word

Look at the word.
Say the word.
Think about the word.
Write the word.
Check the spelling.

322

Name_____

My Study List

1. _____

2. _____

3. _____

4. _____

5. _____

6. _____

7. _____

8. _____

9. _____

10. _____

Review Words

1. frog
2. slip

How to Study a Word

Look at the word.
Say the word.
Think about the word.
Write the word.
Check the spelling.

322

Nature Walk
Spelling Review

Spelling Words

1. these	11. add
2. use	12. mess
3. swim	13. egg
4. glad	14. hope
5. club	15. trip
6. all	16. stone
7. bone	17. lost
8. cute	18. off
9. next	19. grass
10. brave	20. hill

Challenge Words

1. drove
2. mule
3. space
4. storm
5. across

My Study List
Add your own spelling words on the back. ➡

Around the Pond:
Who's Been Here?

Words with Double Consonants
be**ll**, o**ff**, me**ss**, a**dd**, e**gg**

Spelling Words

1. bell	6. hill
2. off	7. well
3. all	8. egg
4. mess	9. will
5. add	10. grass

Challenge Words

1. across
2. skill

My Study List
Add your own spelling words on the back. ➡

Take-Home Word List

Name_____

My Study List

1. _____
2. _____
3. _____
4. _____
5. _____
6. _____
7. _____
8. _____
9. _____
10. _____

Review Words

1. shell
2. kiss

How to Study a Word

Look at the word.
Say the word.
Think about the word.
Write the word.
Check the spelling.

Take-Home Word List

Name_____

My Study List

1. _____
2. _____
3. _____
4. _____
5. _____
6. _____
7. _____
8. _____
9. _____
10. _____

How to Study a Word

Look at the word.
Say the word.
Think about the word.
Write the word.
Check the spelling.

Around Town:

Neighborhood and Community Reading-Writing Workshop

Look carefully at how these words are spelled.

Chinatown

Words Spelled with *th*, *wh*, *sh*, or *ch*

the **th** sound	➡	**th**en, tee**th**
the **wh** sound	➡	**wh**en
the **sh** sound	➡	**sh**eep, di**sh**
the **ch** sound	➡	**ch**ase, tea**ch**

Spelling Words

1. write
2. of
3. do
4. to
5. time
6. went
7. myself
8. what
9. name
10. too
11. little
12. been

Challenge Words

1. right
2. thought

Spelling Words

1. when
2. sheep
3. both
4. then
5. chase
6. teeth
7. teach
8. dish
9. which
10. than
11. wash
12. catch

Challenge Words

1. lunch
2. whistle

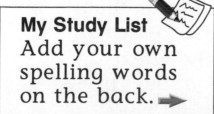

My Study List
Add your own
spelling words
on the back. ➡

My Study List
Add your own
spelling words
on the back. ➡

Take-Home Word List

Name_____

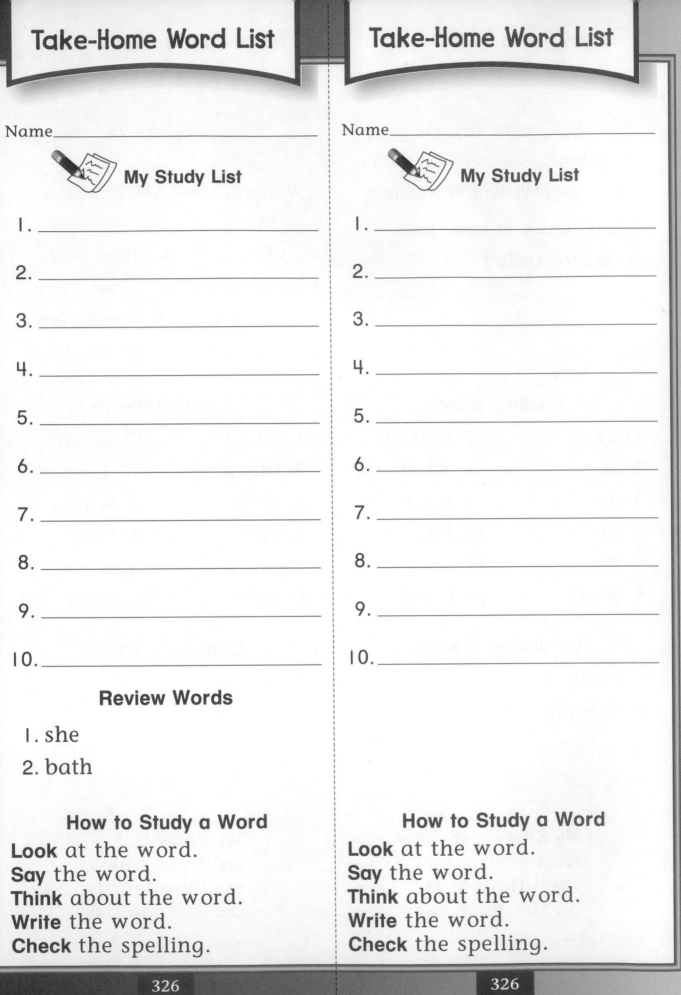

My Study List

1. _____
2. _____
3. _____
4. _____
5. _____
6. _____
7. _____
8. _____
9. _____
10. _____

Review Words

1. she
2. bath

How to Study a Word

Look at the word.
Say the word.
Think about the word.
Write the word.
Check the spelling.

Take-Home Word List

Name_____

My Study List

1. _____
2. _____
3. _____
4. _____
5. _____
6. _____
7. _____
8. _____
9. _____
10. _____

How to Study a Word

Look at the word.
Say the word.
Think about the word.
Write the word.
Check the spelling.

Big Bushy Mustache

The Vowel Sound in *cow*

ow → t**ow**n

ou → h**ou**se

Spelling Words

1. town
2. house
3. sour
4. frown
5. cow
6. clown
7. found
8. how
9. mouse
10. brown
11. could
12. should

Challenge Words

1. around
2. towel

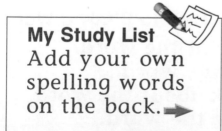

My Study List
Add your own spelling words on the back. →

A Trip to the Firehouse

More Long *a* Spellings

long **a** sound → tr**ay**

tr**ai**n

Spelling Words

1. train
2. tray
3. mail
4. play
5. trail
6. pay
7. sail
8. hay
9. nail
10. rain
11. they
12. great

Challenge Words

1. snail
2. subway

My Study List
Add your own spelling words on the back. →

Take-Home Word List

Name_____

My Study List

1. _____
2. _____
3. _____
4. _____
5. _____
6. _____
7. _____
8. _____
9. _____
10. _____

Review Words

1. stay
2. day

How to Study a Word

Look at the word.
Say the word.
Think about the word.
Write the word.
Check the spelling.

328

Take-Home Word List

Name_____

My Study List

1. _____
2. _____
3. _____
4. _____
5. _____
6. _____
7. _____
8. _____
9. _____
10. _____

Review Words

1. out
2. now

How to Study a Word

Look at the word.
Say the word.
Think about the word.
Write the word.
Check the spelling.

328

Around Town:
Neighborhood and Community
Spelling Review

Spelling Words

1. which
2. teach
3. wash
4. tray
5. frown
6. we
7. eat
8. when
9. teeth
10. sheep
11. sail
12. found
13. be
14. tree
15. chase
16. than
17. play
18. train
19. mouse
20. please

Challenge Words

1. lunch
2. whistle
3. snail
4. around
5. steep

My Study List
Add your own spelling words on the back. ➡

Jamaica Louise James

More Long *e* Spellings

long **e** sound ➡ w**e**
ke**e**p
cl**ea**n

Spelling Words

1. clean
2. keep
3. please
4. feel
5. we
6. be
7. eat
8. tree
9. mean
10. read
11. the
12. people

Challenge Words

1. stream
2. steep

My Study List
Add your own spelling words on the back. ➡

Name_____

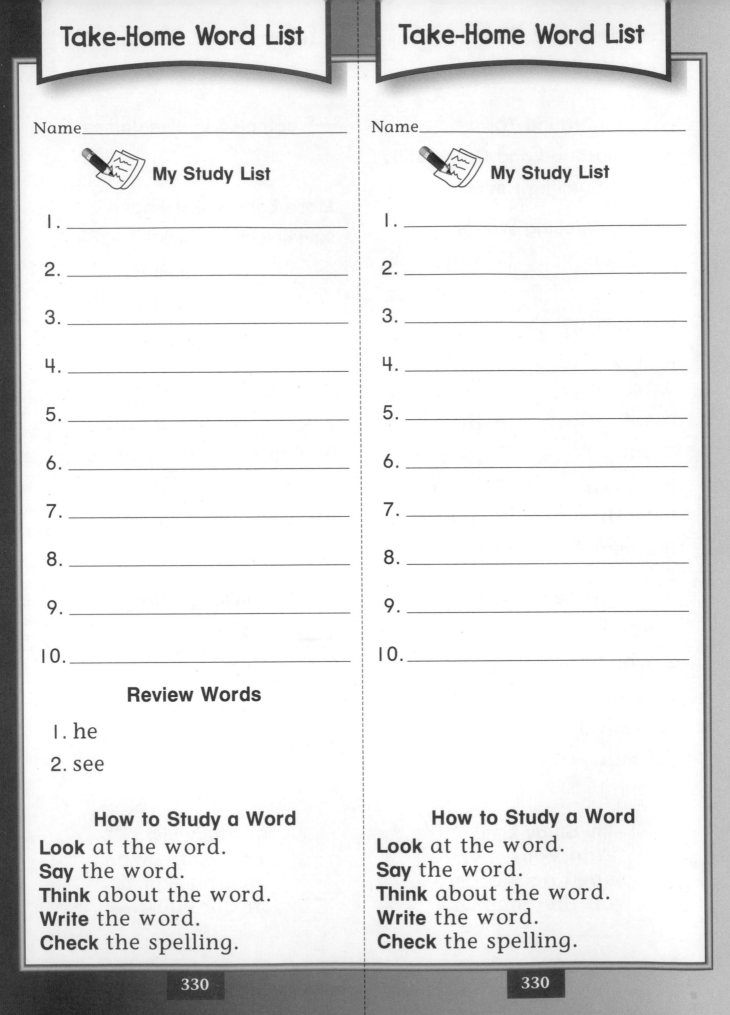 **My Study List**

1._____
2._____
3._____
4._____
5._____
6._____
7._____
8._____
9._____
10._____

Review Words

1. he
2. see

How to Study a Word

Look at the word.
Say the word.
Think about the word.
Write the word.
Check the spelling.

Name_____

My Study List

1._____
2._____
3._____
4._____
5._____
6._____
7._____
8._____
9._____
10._____

How to Study a Word

Look at the word.
Say the word.
Think about the word.
Write the word.
Check the spelling.

Focus on Fables

Words Ending with **k** and **ck**		
Ends with **k** + **e**	➤	la**ke**
Ends with **ck**	➤	ne**ck**
Ends with **k**	➤	as**k**

Spelling Words

1. neck
2. lake
3. sick
4. ask
5. lick
6. pack
7. woke
8. kick
9. lock
10. poke

Challenge Words

1. package
2. wreck

My Study List
Add your own spelling words on the back. ➤

Focus on Poetry

short **a** sound	➤	**a**t, l**a**p
short **e** sound	➤	b**e**d, b**e**nd
short **i** sound	➤	**i**t, w**i**n
short **o** sound	➤	**o**n, st**o**p
short **u** sound	➤	**u**s, m**u**st
long **a** sound	➤	m**a**ke
long **i** sound	➤	k**i**te

Spelling Words

1. pal
2. skip
3. dime
4. just
5. tape
6. bump
7. wipe
8. yet
9. wide
10. pile

Challenge Words

1. huge
2. whisk

My Study List
Add your own spelling words on the back. ➤

Take-Home Word List

Name_____

My Study List

1. _____
2. _____
3. _____
4. _____
5. _____
6. _____
7. _____
8. _____
9. _____
10. _____

Review Words

1. gave
2. like

How to Study a Word

Look at the word.
Say the word.
Think about the word.
Write the word.
Check the spelling.

Take-Home Word List

Name_____

My Study List

1. _____
2. _____
3. _____
4. _____
5. _____
6. _____
7. _____
8. _____
9. _____
10. _____

Review Words

1. take
2. make

How to Study a Word

Look at the word.
Say the word.
Think about the word.
Write the word.
Check the spelling.

332

Read each question. Check your paper for each kind of mistake. Correct any mistakes you find.

☐ Did I begin each sentence with a capital letter?

☐ Did I use the correct end mark?

☐ Did I spell each word correctly?

☐ Did I indent each paragraph?

Proofreading Marks		
∧	Add one or more words.	want to I see the play. ∧
—	Take out one or more words. Change the spelling.	The boat ~~did~~ moved slowly. filled The cloud ~~filed~~ the sky.
/	Make a capital letter a small letter.	The A̸nimals hid from the storm.
≡	Make a small letter a capital letter.	There are thirty days in a̲pril.

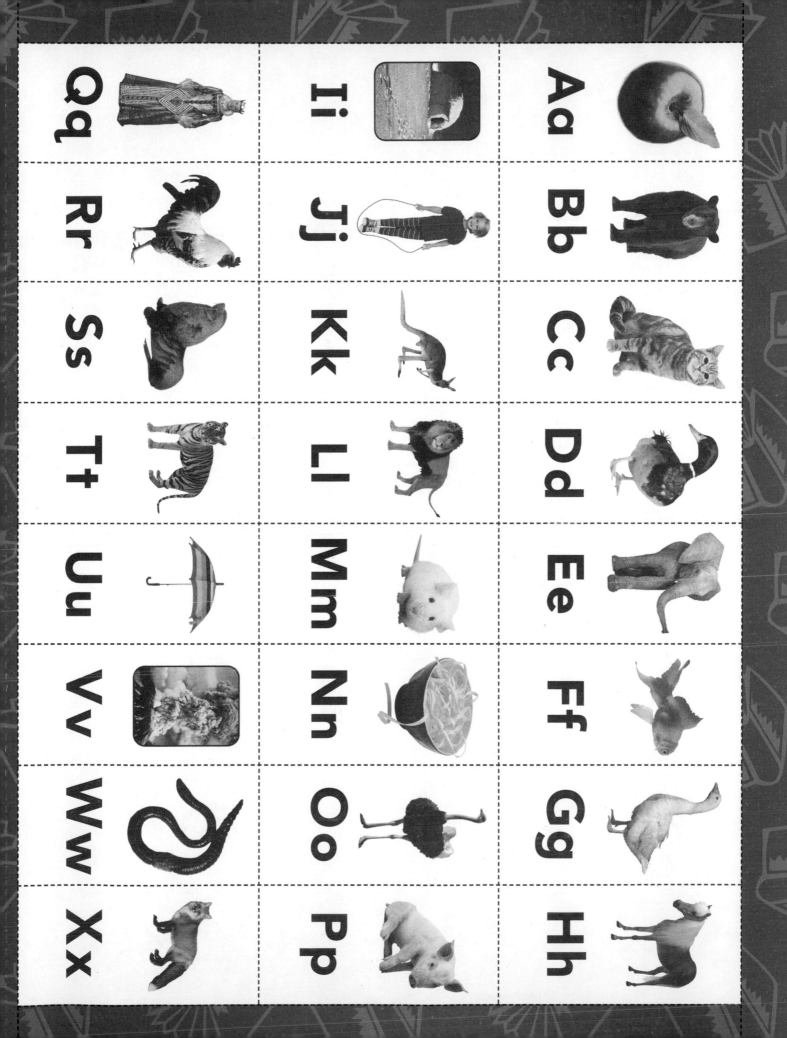

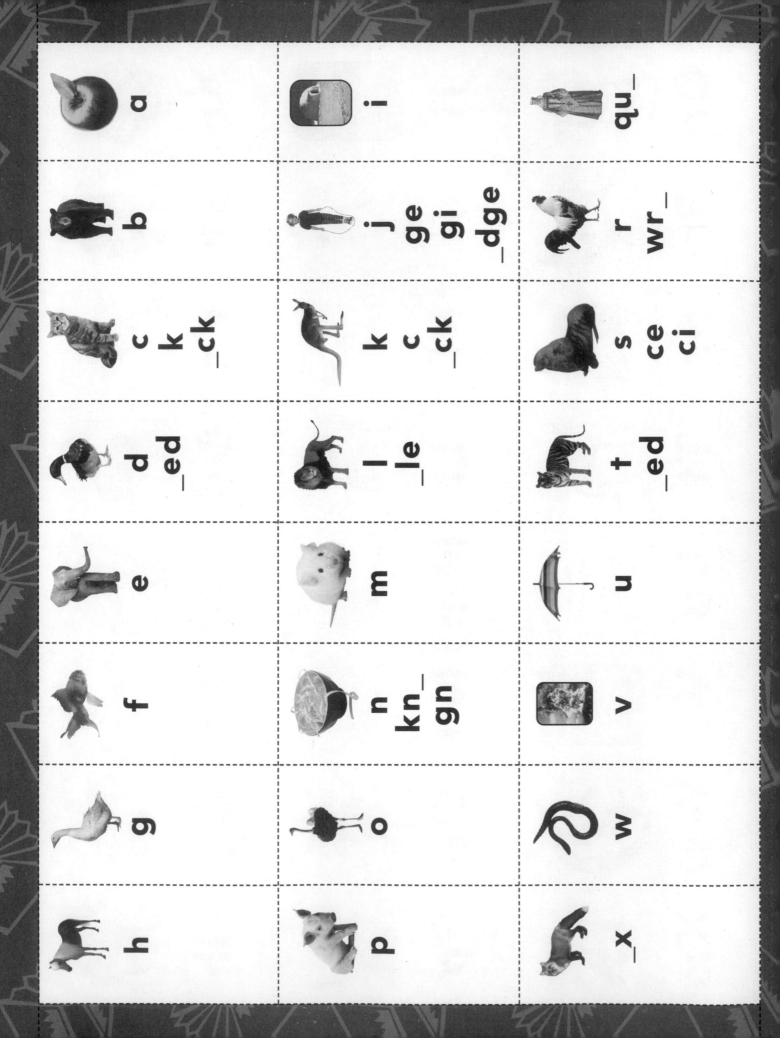

a

b

c
k
_ck

d
_ed

e

f

g

h

i

j
ge
gi
_dge

k
c
_ck

l
_le

m

n
kn_
gn

o

p

qu_

r
wr_

s
ce
ci

t
_ed

u

v

w

_x

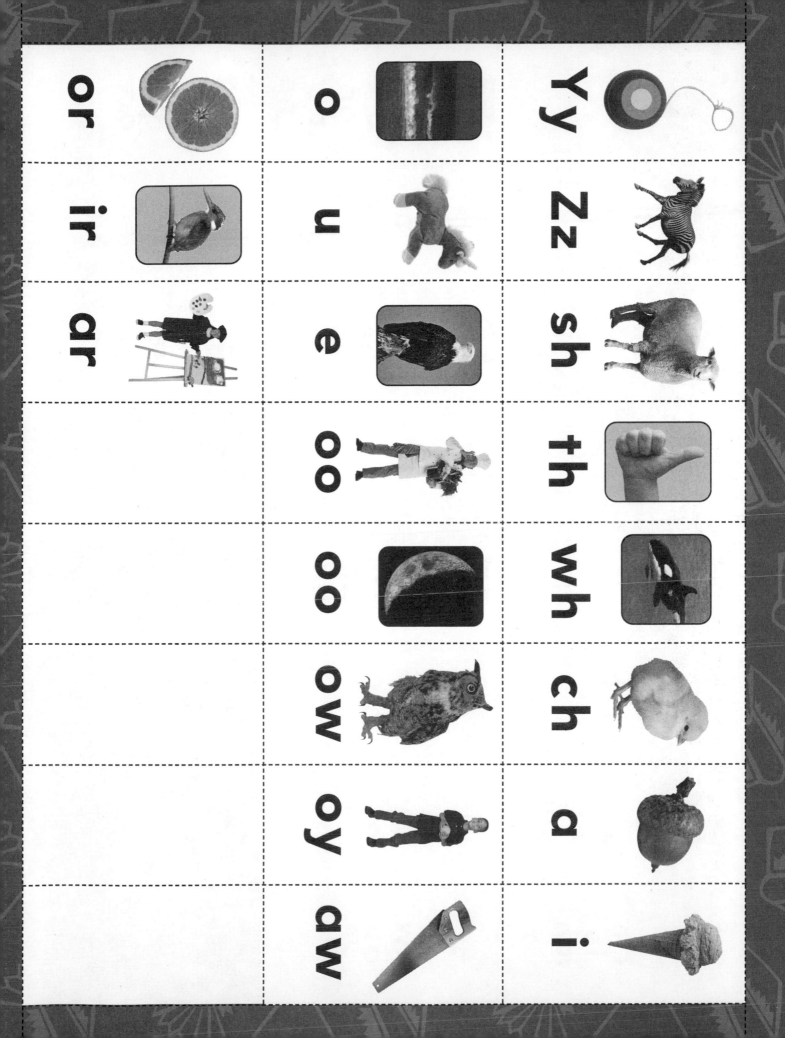

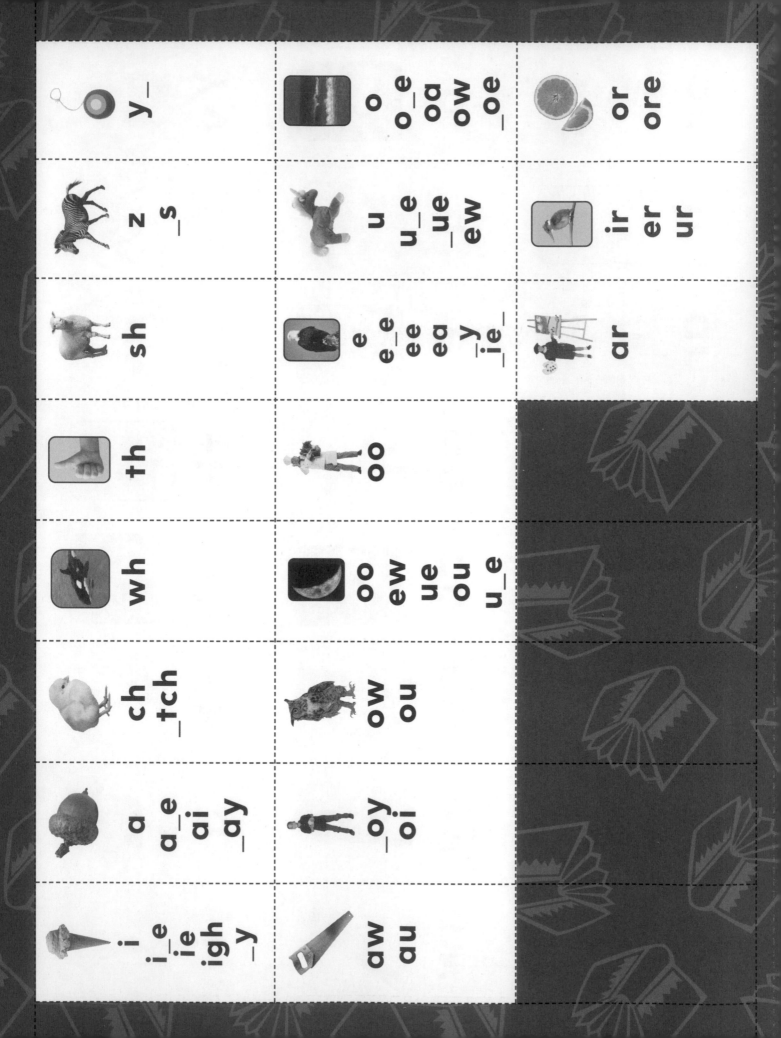

y _

o
o_e
oa
ow
_oe

or
ore

z
_s

u
u_e
_ue
ew

ir
er
ur

sh

e
e_e
ee
ea
_y
ie_

ar

th

oo

wh

oo
ew
ue
ou
u_e

ch
_tch

ow
ou

a
a_e
ai
_ay

_oy
oi

i
i_e
_ie
igh
_y

aw
au

A	A	A	B	B	C	C	D	D
E	E	E	F	F	G	G	H	H
I	I	J	J	K	K	L	L	M
M	N	N	O	O	P	P	Q	Q
R	R	S	S	T	T	U	U	V
V	W	W	X	X	Y	Y	Z	Z

You can add punctuation marks or other letters to the blanks.

Letter Tray

⬇

Letter Tray

c a t

fold

fold

fold

d	d	c	c	b	b	a	a	a
h	h	g	g	f	f	e	e	e
m	l	l	k	k	j	j	i	i
q	q	p	p	o	o	n	n	m
v	u	u	t	t	s	s	r	r
z	z	y	y	x	x	w	w	v

fold

fold

fold

Henry and Mudge and the Starry Night	Mrs. Brown Went to Town	Dragon Gets By
beautiful	different	bought
even	floor	front
quiet	letter	kitchen
straight	move	roll
year	poor	until
	word	Julius
		brought
		reason
		special
		surprise

You can add your own words for sentence building.

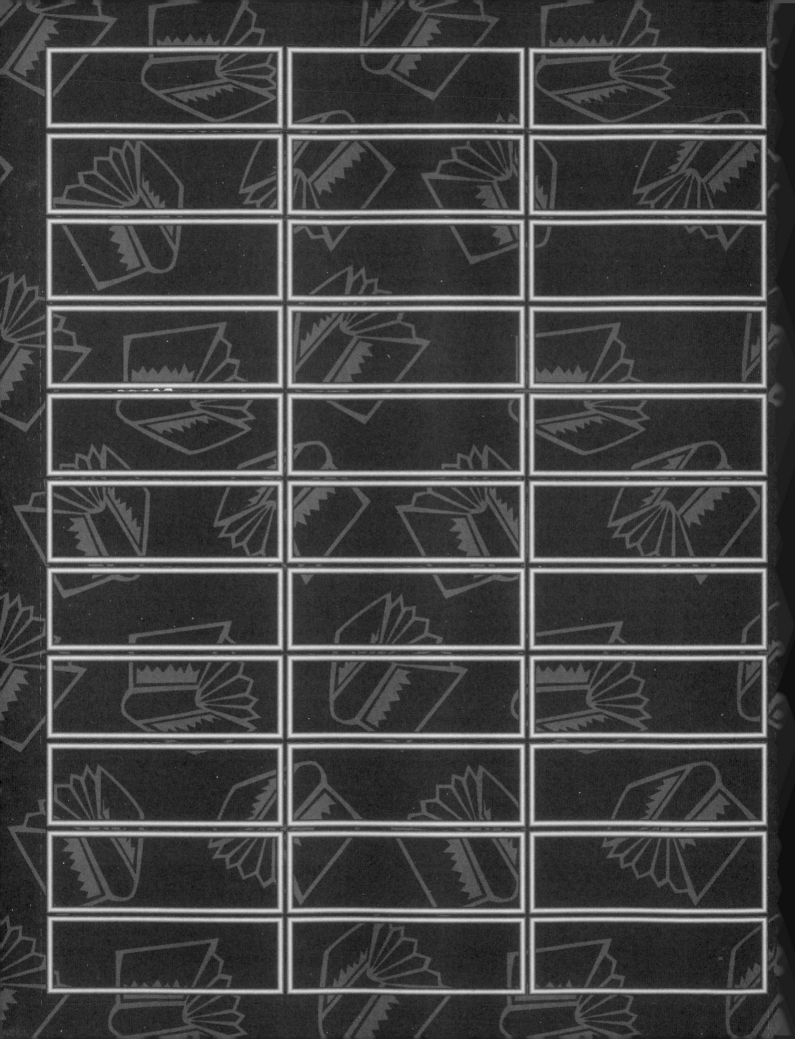

Name _____

Match the Opposites

Draw a line from each word on the left to a word on the right that has the opposite meaning.

1. sad	found
2. lost	finish
3. never	happy
4. thick	thin
5. below	always
6. start	above

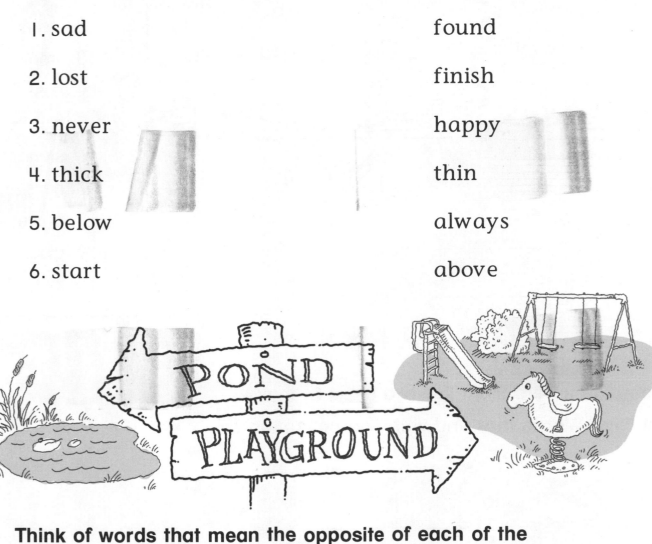

Think of words that mean the opposite of each of the words below. Write those words on the lines.

7. front _____   9. dark _____

8. soft _____   10. asleep _____

Spelling Spree

**Combine letters from the two frogs to make the
Spelling Words that begin with two consonants.**

tr sw st
cl br gl

ip im ep ad
ub one ave

1. trip
2. swim
3. step
4. nest
5. club
6. stone
7. next
8. brave
9. glad
10. lost

1. _____

2. _____

3. _____

4. _____

5. _____

6. _____

7. _____

**Combine letters from the two birds to make
Spelling Words that end with two consonants.**

ne lo

st xt

8. _____

9. _____

10. _____